SOUR MjLK CURDS
the white love stain
logan benedict

Sour Milk Curds (The White Love Stain)
Copyright © 2018 by Logan Benedict
All rights reserved
ISBN: 1986040593
ISBN-13: 978-1986040594

THIS IS FOR THE ONES I LOVE

FOR THE ONES I LOST

FOR THE ONES WHO HURT MOST

AND FOR WHOM I GRIEVE

FEBRUARY 9 2017
9:37 PM

ALL THE MEN i MEET DiSAPPEAR iNTO THiN AiR
THEY DiSSOLVE LiKE SALT iN WATER iN AiR iN LiGHT
FEiGN AN iNTEREST THEN DROP MY BODY LiKE BRiCKS
    OFF A BRiDGE
SPEND MY TiME WASTE MY TiME THROW THE CLOCK
    AWAY
MAKE ME FEEL ELECTRiC THEN DOUSE ME iN WATER

i'M NOT WHAT YOU WANT i'M NOT THAT MAN
i FEEL LiKE i'M NOTHiNG iF NOT THE ENEMY

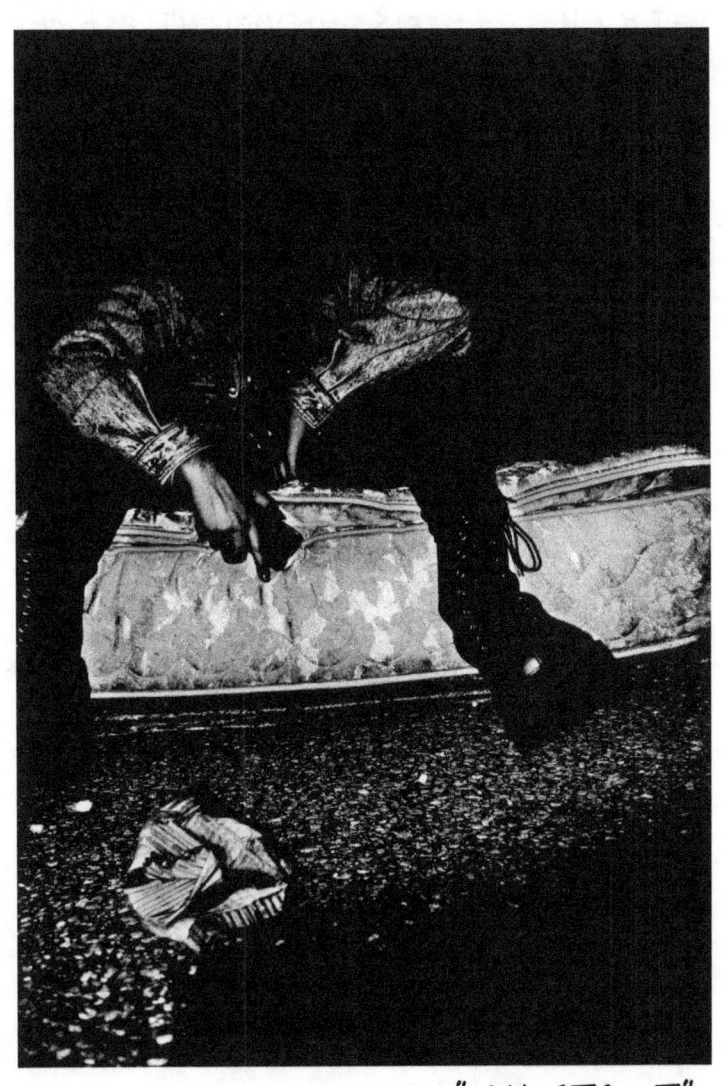

"96th STREET"
FEBRUARY 23 2017

FEBRUARY 16 2017
3:41 PM

DUNCE CAP ON
WITH MY HIGH HEELS AND VIOLENT RED CHEEKS
SCREAMING BUCKTOOTHED NAKED GRIN
LIKE A DIRTY MUDDY ANGEL

MARCH 4 2017
1:22 AM

I DON'T SLEEP
I WRAP MY FINGERS IN ROPE UNTIL ALL CIRCULATION IS
    LOST
CARESSING THE COLD CORPSE
KEEPING MY EYES OPEN TO ALL THE PAIN I'M FEELING
SCRAPING MY KNEES ON THE CONCRETE WILLINGLY AGAIN
EVADING ALL CONTACT
FOR A FIGHTING CHANCE
AND I WILL BURN DOWN EVERY AMERICAN FLAG I FIND

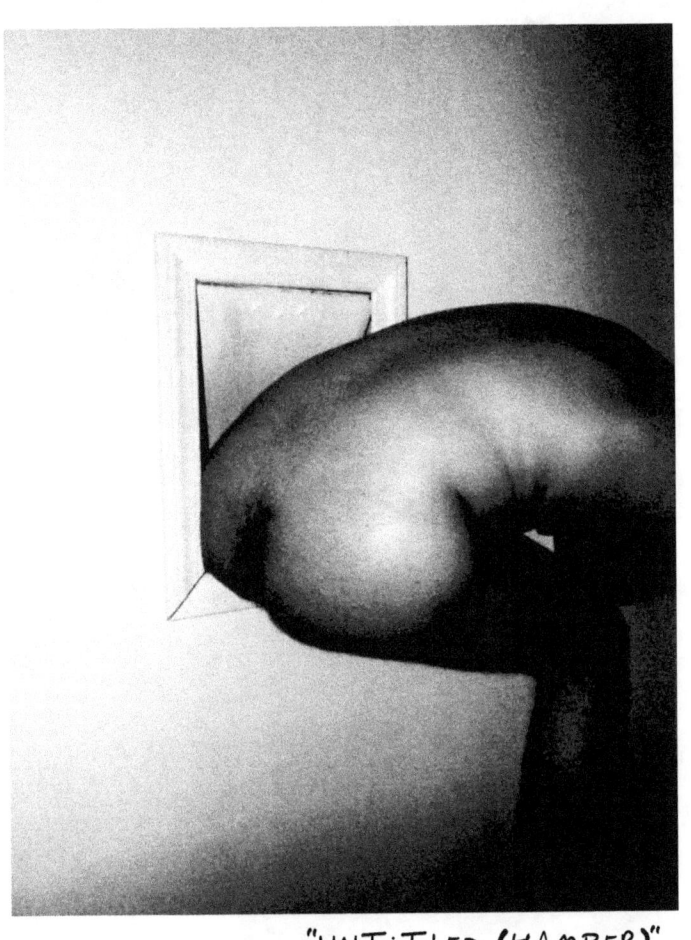

"UNTITLED (HAMPER)"
APRIL 29 2017

MARCH 17 2017
12:25 AM

A CITY MARRED WITH SCARS AND BLESSED WITH KISSES
HE WAS THE KNIFE AND THE BANDAGE
AND I SAW THE CITY LIGHTS AND I WANTED TO TURN
    THEM ALL OFF

MARCH 19 2017
2:53 PM

LOVE IS A SAVAGE MIRROR SWITCHBLADE SOUR SWEET
FUCKING TO THE SOUND OF THE CITY
SIRENS WAILING AND INCESSANT HORNS HONKING AND
    PEDESTRIAN CHATTER
MY ACID WASHED TONGUE TIED
SLEEPING IN THE WAR ZONE WITH A DEADPAN PULSE

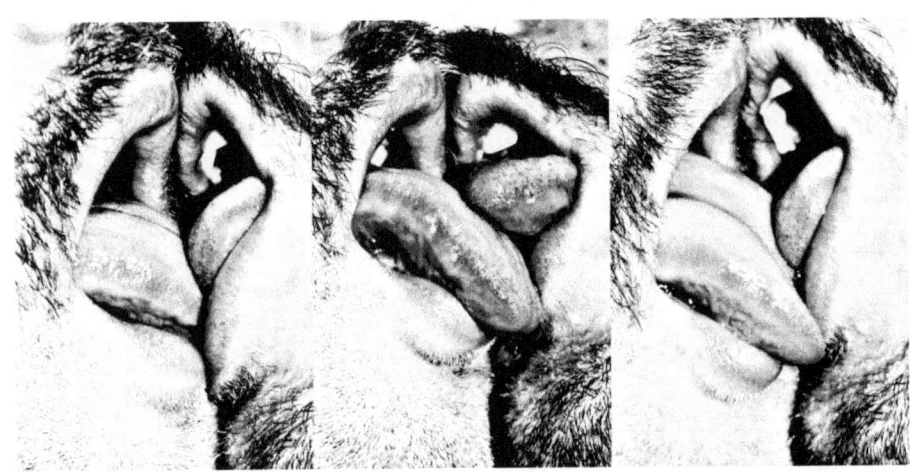
"THE PERFECT MOMENT"
MARCH 27 2017

MARCH 30 2017
12:25 PM

MY DANGEROUS PAST TIMES KEEP GRASSY PATCHES ON
    MY SPINE
MAKE MY EYES OPEN WIDE TO THE SIGHTS YOU OFFER
WIRES WINCE AND COIL AROUND MY WRISTS AND NECK
AND MY HEAD GROWS HEAVY ON THESE WEAK
    SHOULDERS
ALL A REMINDER FOR THE WORSE BATS OF EYELASHES

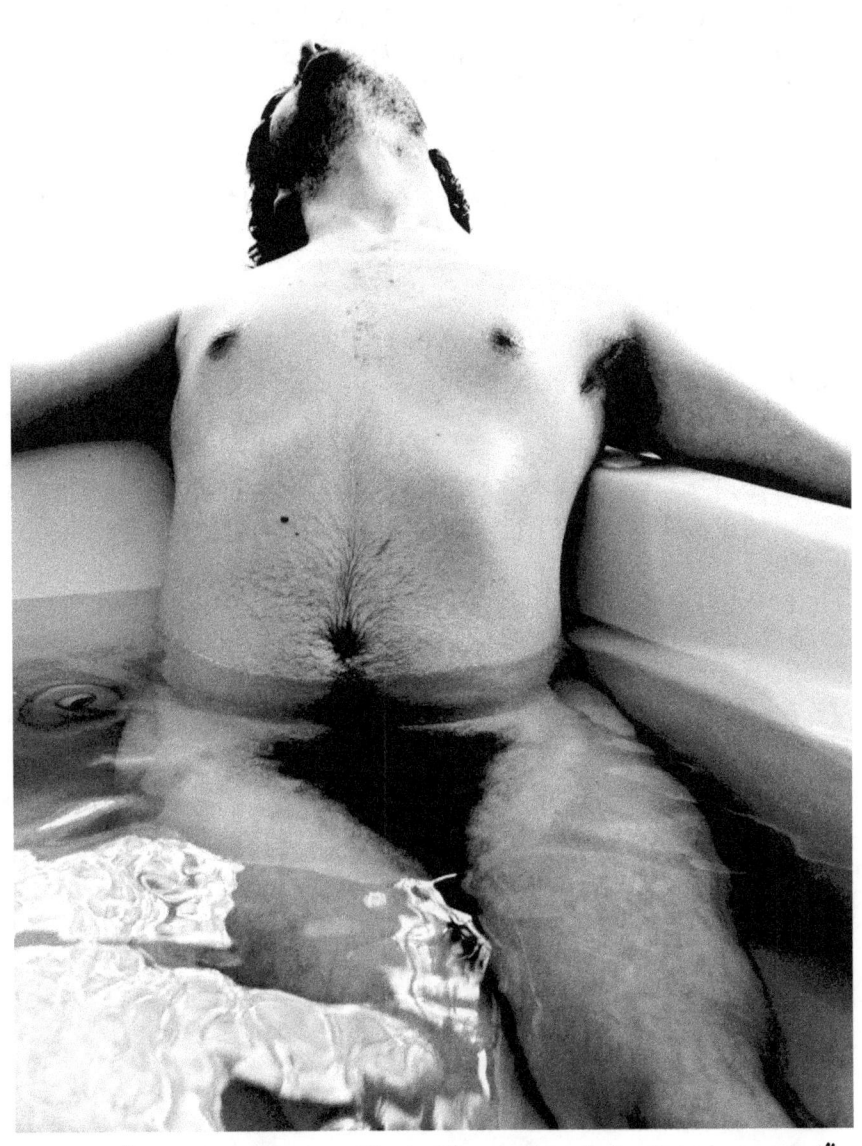

APRIL 4 2017
12:18 AM

i CRY SOFTLY WEARING MY LUCKY CRYSTAL EARRING
BLOOD AND SWEAT AND SALIVA AS LUBRICANT AGAIN
THE TRAUMATICS OF A LOVE UNWARRANTED
HE LAUGHS LIKE A GUNMAN AND TASTES LIKE A MARY
CLIMAXING WITHOUT INVITATION

TO BE NOTHING BUT AN OBJECT
A TIGHT HOLE BENT OVER YOUR KITCHEN COUNTER

APRIL 6 2017
1:25 PM

WE FUCK TO GENESIS
HE TASTES LIKE WEED AND TOBACCO AND RUM BUT HIS
    LIPS ARE GENTLE AND PROMISING SOMETHING
TWO TIMES CAME
THE NAKED NURSE
SLIDES ON THE COCK RING
TORAH ON THE TELEVISION
HE ENTERS ME AND MY BODY BECOMES NUMB
HE STAYS INSIDE
HIS WIRY, HAIRY BODY ON TOP OF MY OWN

THE CRYSTALS HAVE SHADOWS TODAY
AND I DON'T WANT HIM TO TELL ME TO LEAVE
I WANT TO SLEEP IN HIS ARMS
GET LOST IN HIS CHEST HAIR

APRIL 13 2017
8:54 AM

i WANT TO BE YOUR ARM CANDY
YOUR GOOD NIGHT'S REST
YOUR MORNING DELIGHT
YOURS

i WANT TO BE YOUR ECSTASY
YOUR GRUNT AND RELEASE
YOUR CATACOMB

i JUST WANT YOU TO STICK AROUND AFTER YOU CUM
AND i WANT TO FEEL YOUR HANDS ON MY COLD BODY
    INTIMATELY HOVERING OVER MY ORGANS
SOOTHING MY NERVES

APRIL 18 2017
8:30 PM

i WAKE HiM UP WiTH A PHONE CALL
THEN WE FUCK UNDER CHRiSTMAS STRiNGS
THiGHS BROWN MUDDY WiTHOUT A FiGHT
WiTHOUT DEFiNiTiON

i SPiT BLOOD FROM MY MOUTH
SiGHiNG SOUR TOOTH
WiTH NO HAND ON MY BREAST

HE'LL USE ANY EXCUSE FOR ME TO LEAVE HiS BED AFTER
    HE GETS HiS ROCKS OFF
HE WON'T TOUCH ME UNTiL i'M GONE
i'M NOT HiS FRiEND i'M NOT HiS LOVER
i WOULD RATHER BE DEAD THAN CONTiNUE THiS HURT

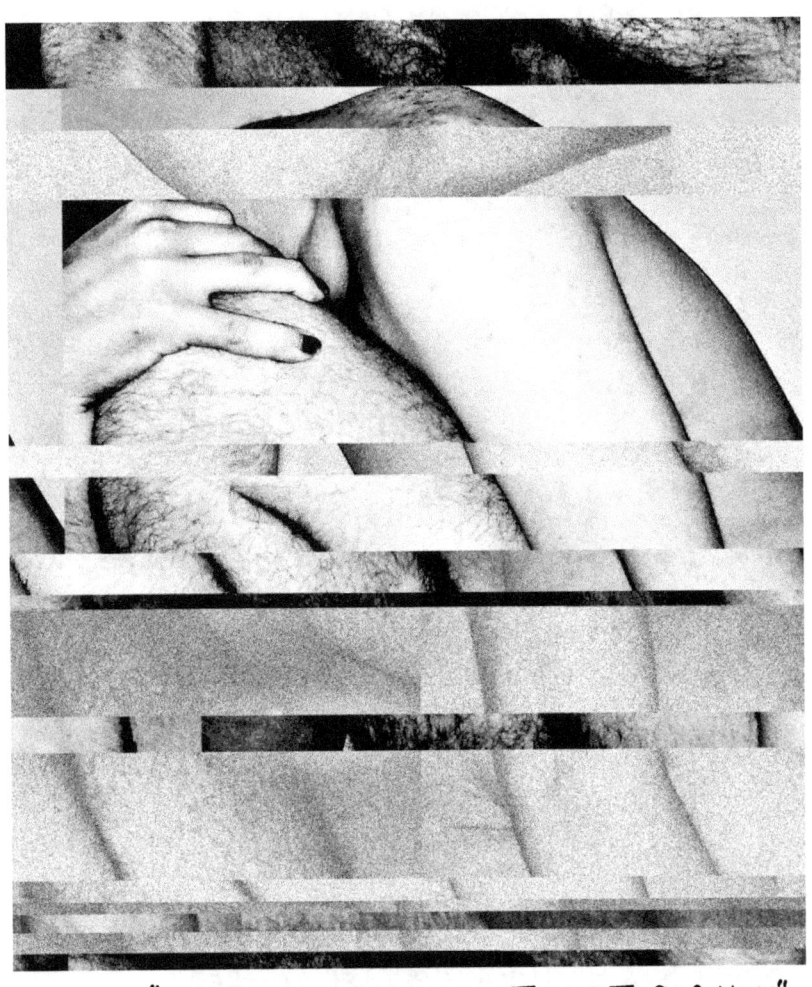

"i MAR MY BODY iN CONTEMPT FOR YOU"
JULY 5 2017

APRIL 26 2017
11:46 PM

i WANT BACK MY VIRGINITY
i WANT TO PRY iT OUT OF YOUR HAiRY PALMS AND
    RETURN iT TO MY SANCTUARY
i WANT TO TAKE iT BACK FROM THE MATTRESS ON
    THE FLOOR OF YOUR BEDROOM WiTH THE SHEETS
    OFF THE EDGES
i WANT TO RETRiEVE MY SCREAMS AND CRiES FROM
    THE PiLLOW THAT COVERED MY MOUTH THERE
i WANT TO CLEAN MY iNSiDES OF THE PEARLY HONEY
    YOU DRiPPED iNSiDE
i WANT TO EXORCiSE MY BRAiN FROM THE VERY
    MEMORY OF YOUR NONCHALANT iNEBRiATED
    SMiLE, THAT MUSTACHED GRiN WiTH THiCK
    FRAMED GLASSES AND CURLY LOCKS
i WANT TO BE MYSELF AGAiN WiTHOUT THE ANXiETY
    OR PANiC OF DiSEASE
i WANT TO SET MYSELF ABLAZE WiTH CONTENTiON
    WiTH FURY, MY ONE SiDED ARGUMENT, MY iNNER
    STRUGGLE
YOU NEVER KNEW YOU NEVER ASKED YOU NEVER
    WANTED TO KNOW

AND iNSiDE i'M TiGHTLY BOUND AND SCARED iT WAS
    NOTHiNG NEVER ANYTHiNG NOTHiNG TO
    ANYBODY NOTHiNG NOBODY NOBODY
YOU WERE THE THUNDER CLAPPiNG BETWEEN MY
    SPLiNTERED THiGHS
YOU WERE THE STORM i WiSHED AWAY
YOU WERE A HELLUVA HUSTLER FOR REAL

APRIL 27 2017
12:31 PM

i'M NOTHiNG iF NOT BURDENED BY THE MEMORiES OF
    UNRECiPROCATED AFFECTiON AND PERiLS OF
    PHYSiCAL PLEASURE
i'M NOTHiNG iF NOT A SKELETON OF DESiRE, A PACiFiER
    FOR LONELY LOViNG, CRUiSiNG THE HiGHWAYS
i'M NOTHiNG FOR YOU HAVE STRiPPED ME NAKED iN
    YOUR APARTMENT AND YOU'RE HARDER THAN
    HABiTS TO BREAK

COERCED AGAiN
AND MY THiGHS ARE WET FROM THE ViOLATiON
A CARCASS OF PAST COMPASSiON
WiTH A CERTAiNTY TOO MiLD TO BE DECAPiTATiNG
BUT iN MY MiND i'M DRiNKiNG DAGGERS WiTH NO
    CHASER

MY MONEY BURNS iN THE WASTE BiN CLOSELY
NO ALLEGiANCES i HOLD TiGHTLY
MY POiNT WASTED AND UGLY
NONE OF THESE GLUTTONS DESERVE A LAST SUPPER

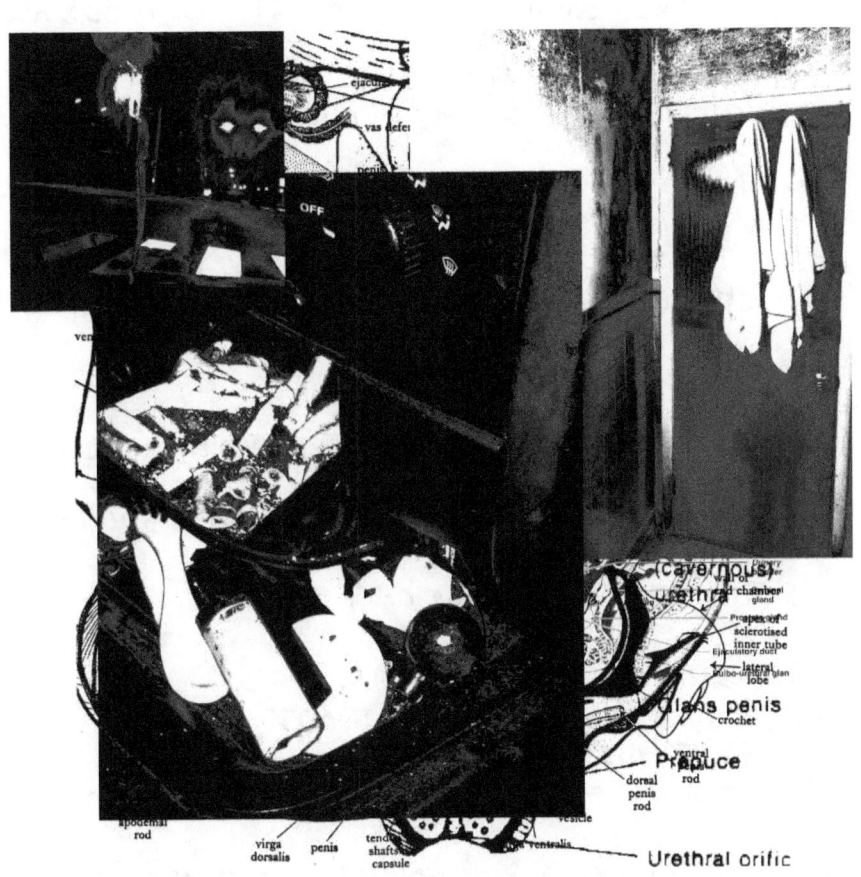

MAY 9 2017
12:17 AM

GEMINI CAME INSIDE AND TASTED THE ENTRYWAY OF
    MY CAVE
WENT AHEAD AND MADE MY DAY
SMOKED SEVEN CIGARETTES AND PUT HIS HANDS ALL
    OVER ME
I TRIED TO DETACH FROM THE SWEATY GLARES BUT I
    KNOW HE WILL BATHE IN CHAOS TONIGHT

THE ORGAN SO ORCHESTRAL SO OMNIPRESENT
SPYING IN ON MY SECRET SORROWS
I HAVE TEARS FOR YEARS AND SAID CONFUSION TO
    CHOKE

HIGH BEAMS ON THE HIGHWAY
RUNNING ME OFF THE ROAD
HIS GAZE SO GRANDIOSE SO GREAT I GIVE HIM FULL
    CONTROL
I CARELESSLY CARESS THE CORPSE KNOWING SOON IT
    WILL BE MINE
HE'S THE SPITTING IMAGE OF THE DEVIL

THERE'S BLOOD UNDER MY NAILS
I TRIED SCRATCHING MY HEART OUT
BECAUSE IT HURTS ME SO BADLY
IT'S NOTHING IF NOT NEVER-ENDING

NOTHING CAN BREAK YOU DOWN LIKE A MAN CAN

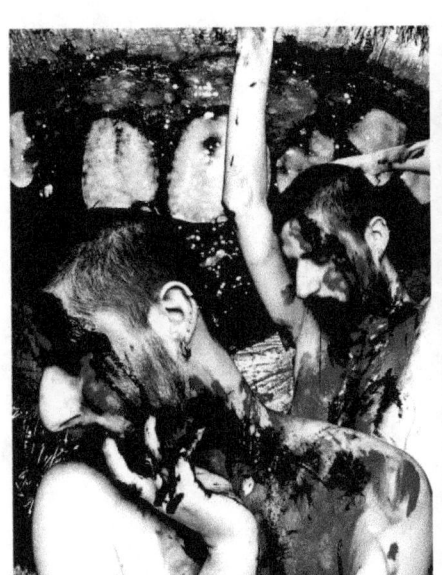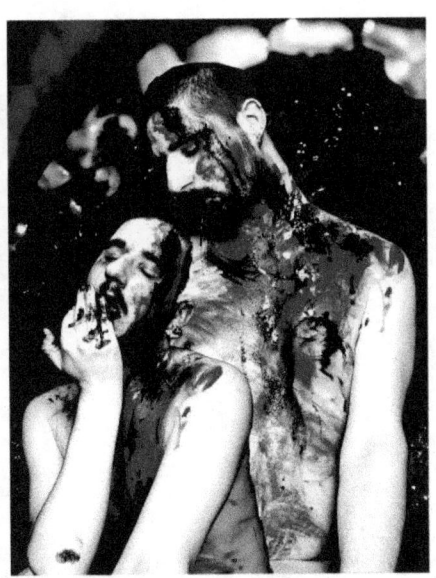

"TOKEN OF TRAUMA"
DECEMBER 4 2017

MAY 24 2017
1:26 PM

THE CALL FALLS TO A QUIET BUZZ
THE NONCHALANCE OF THE TAKER
THE AGONY STILL WET ON MY TONGUE
I'M NAMING BONES AND FEELINGS
BUT THE MEMORY STINGS WHEN I'M WITH ANOTHER

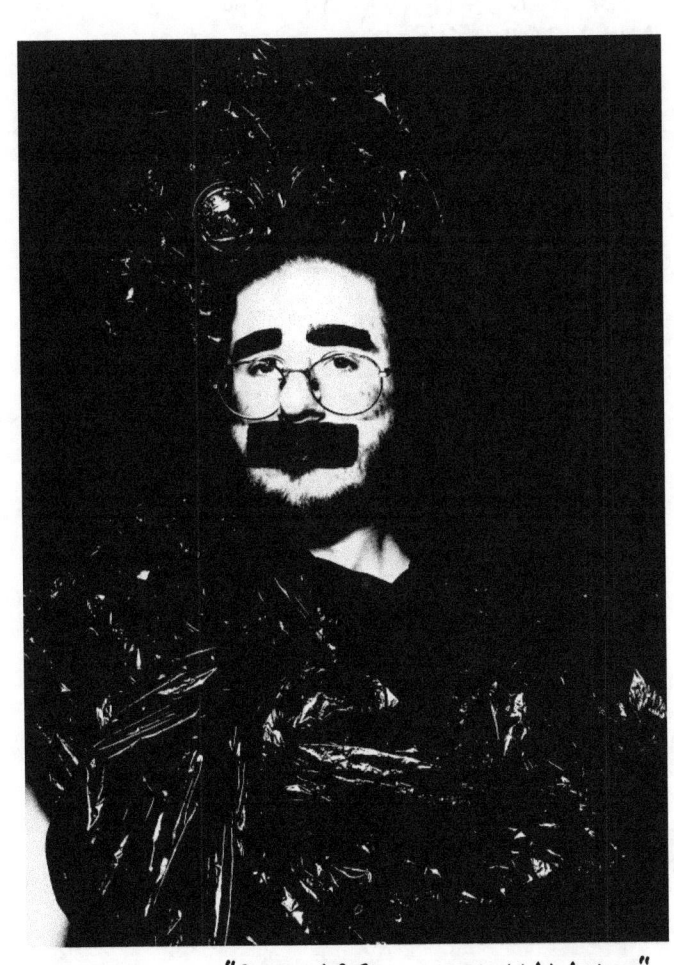

"REHEARSED NONCHALANCE"
MAY 17 2017

JUNE 22 2017
6:30 PM

THE CASUALTY OF A FAILED ROMANCE
WHEN BLOOD CURDLES
YOUR HANDS LEAVE MY SKIN
AND i FALL ASLEEP

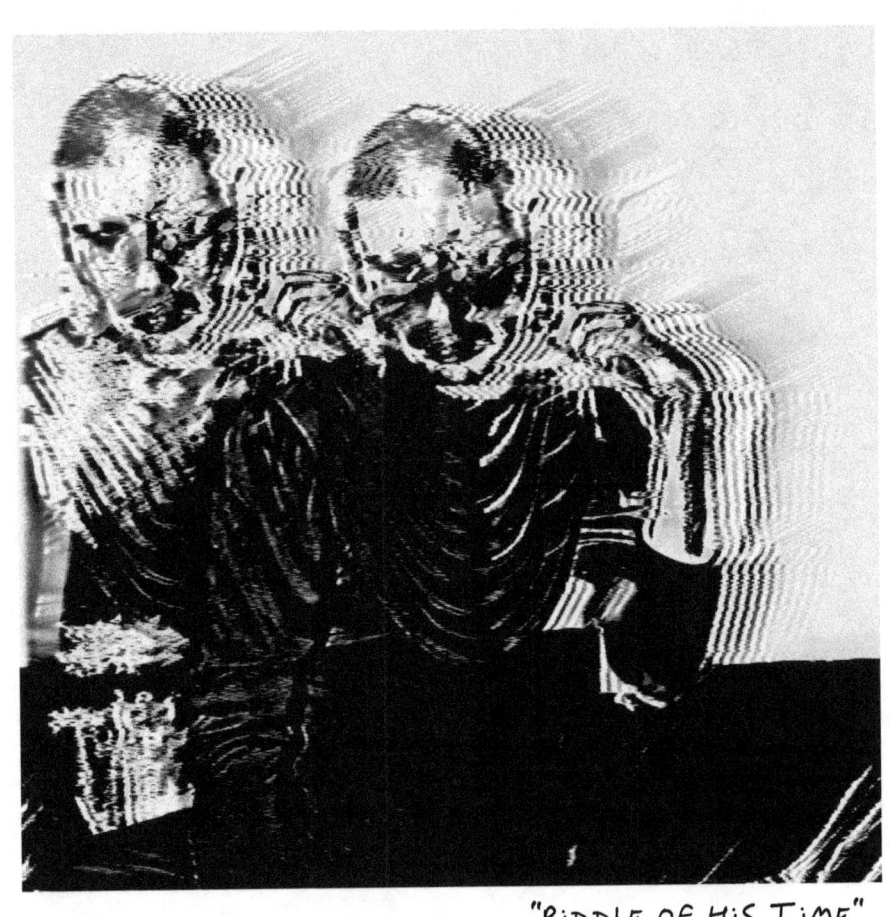

"RIDDLE OF HIS TIME"
JANUARY 9 2018

JULY 1 2017
7:05 PM

HE SMOKES THE TAR
AND CUMS AGAIN
WITH SALT WATER IN HIS EYES
HIS HAND ON MY UPPER THIGH
UNDER PSEUDO PRETENSION

SO LOVE IS A MYTH

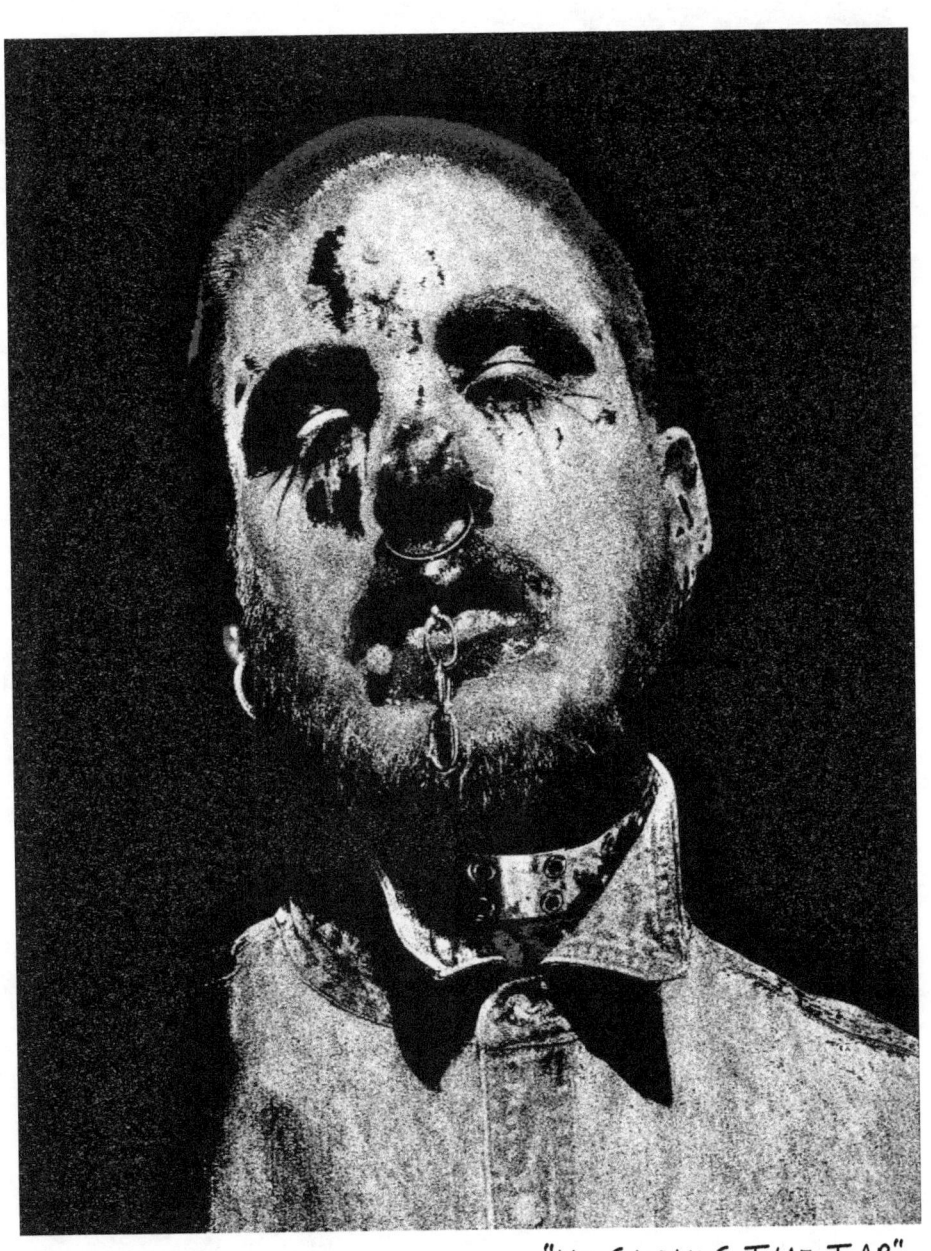

"HE SMOKES THE TAR"
JULY 3 2017

JULY 6 2017
2:45 PM

i WANT TO OCCUPY YOUR MiND
LiKE AN iNSECT CRAWLiNG AROUND iNSiDE YOUR HOLLOW
      SKULL

i WANT TO TASTE THE NECTAR,
THE BUBBLiNG MiLK OF YOUR ROD
AND i WANT TO FUCK YOU FOREVER
BUT i WANT EVERY THOUGHT TO BE MiNE

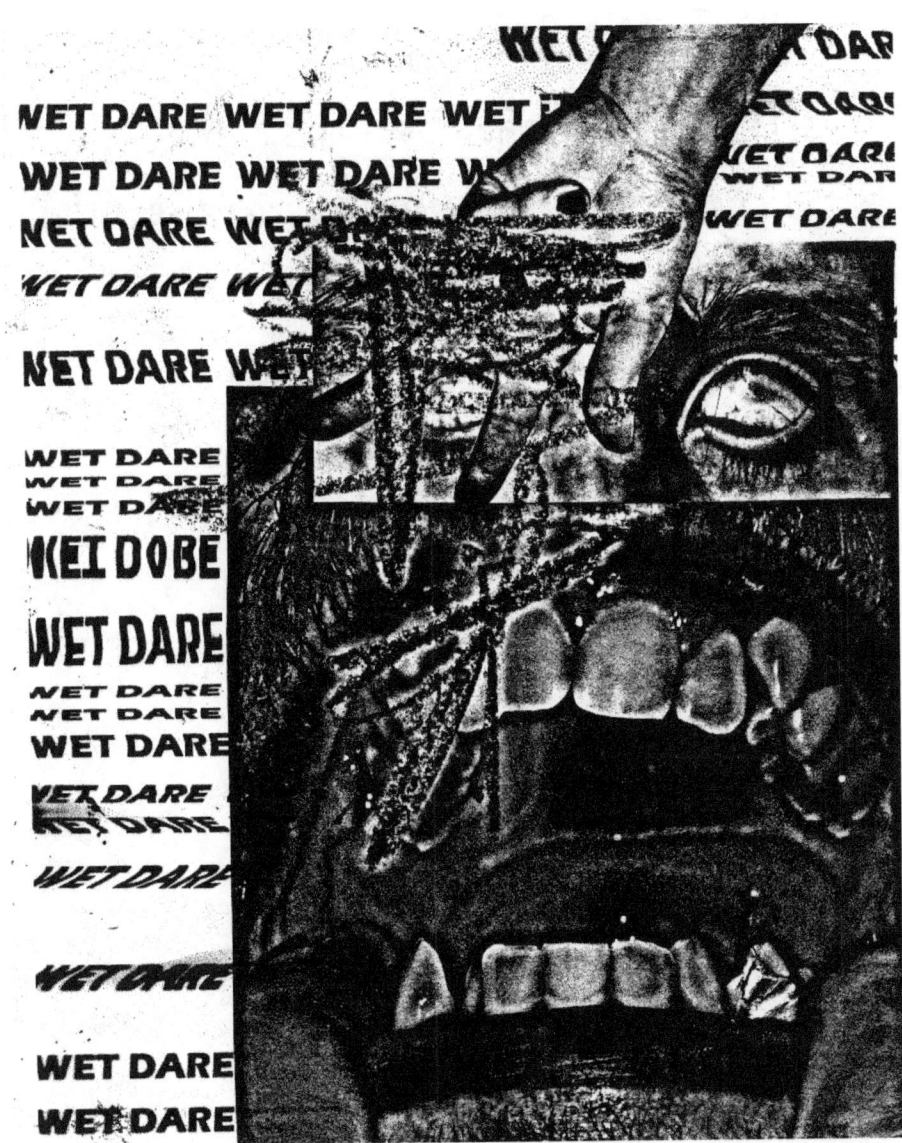

"WET DARE"
DECEMBER 4 2017

JULY 11 2017
11:02 PM

HOW DOES IT FEEL TO KNOW YOU ROBBED ME OF MY
    BODY, MY MIND, MY LOVE?
MILKED THE CORPSE AND FUCKED THE ASS
    REPEATEDLY WITHOUT PERMISSION?

I'M TORTURED BY THE THOUGHTS OF YOUR DRUNK,
    PERSUASIVE SMILE AND STUBBLE,
YOUR CARELESS CARESSES AND GLORIFIED EGO

LOSING MYSELF FOR YOU MADE IT CLEAR
HOW IMPOSSIBLE IS COMPASSION

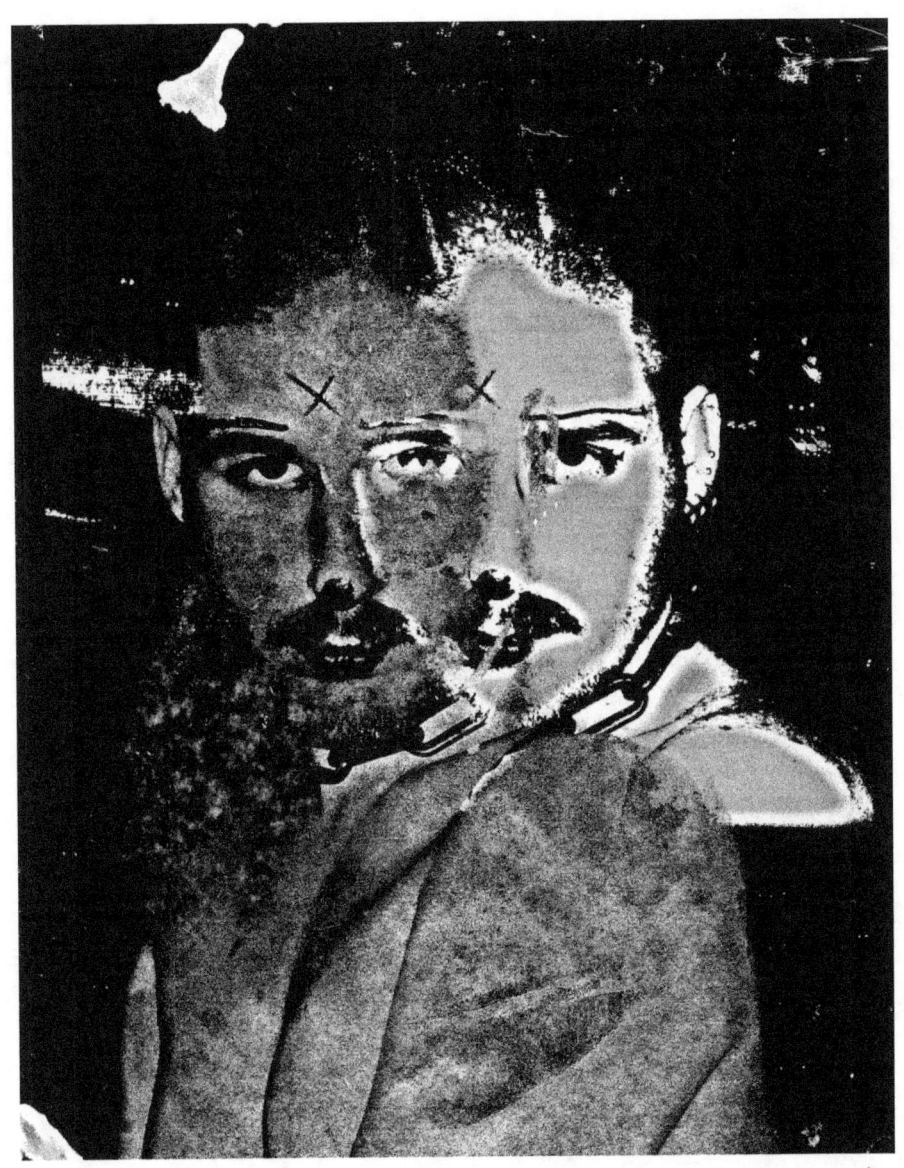
"SOMETIMES THE LOW IS THE HIGH (NO. 1)"
DECEMBER 12 2017

JULY 14 2017
2:19 AM

BIG FAT TEARS
WITH NOTHING BEHIND THE BLOODSHOT
CHALICE FULL OF THE NOISES WE USED TO MAKE

I CARVE THE X INTO MY FORE
I LOSE MY EARRING IN YOUR JUNGLE
AND THERE'S MALICE HERE

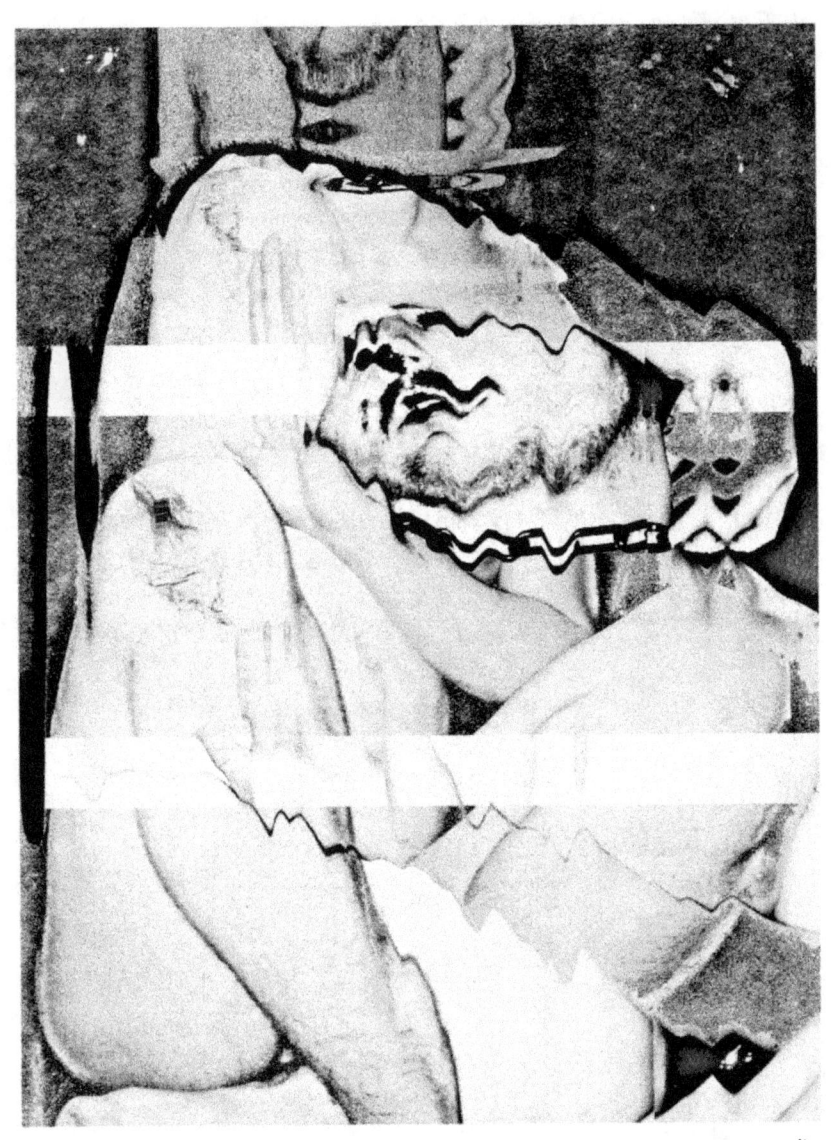

"SOMETIMES THE LOW IS THE HIGH (NO. 2)"
DECEMBER 12 2017

JULY 18 2017
11:40 PM

WITH THE CITY STATIC ON THE TV
HE'S THE RELIEF HE BRINGS THE HEAT
AND SWEAT ON MY BEGGING BONES

DEPARTING NEAR MIDNIGHT WITH BARELY A KISS,
    BARELY AKIN
NAKED IN THE BACKYARD IN A LAWN CHAIR SMOKING
    WITH HIS LONGER HAIR
NOT SOBER BUT A GOD

i DON'T WANT TO RUIN THE SACRAMENT
i WANT TO VISIT THE MONUMENT EVERY WEEK WITH
    YOU
i WANT TO LICK THE SALT FROM YOUR SPINE AND
    WATCH THE ECSTASY DISSOLVE ON YOUR
    TONGUE
i WANT TO SEE MYSELF INSIDE YOUR THICK FRAMES

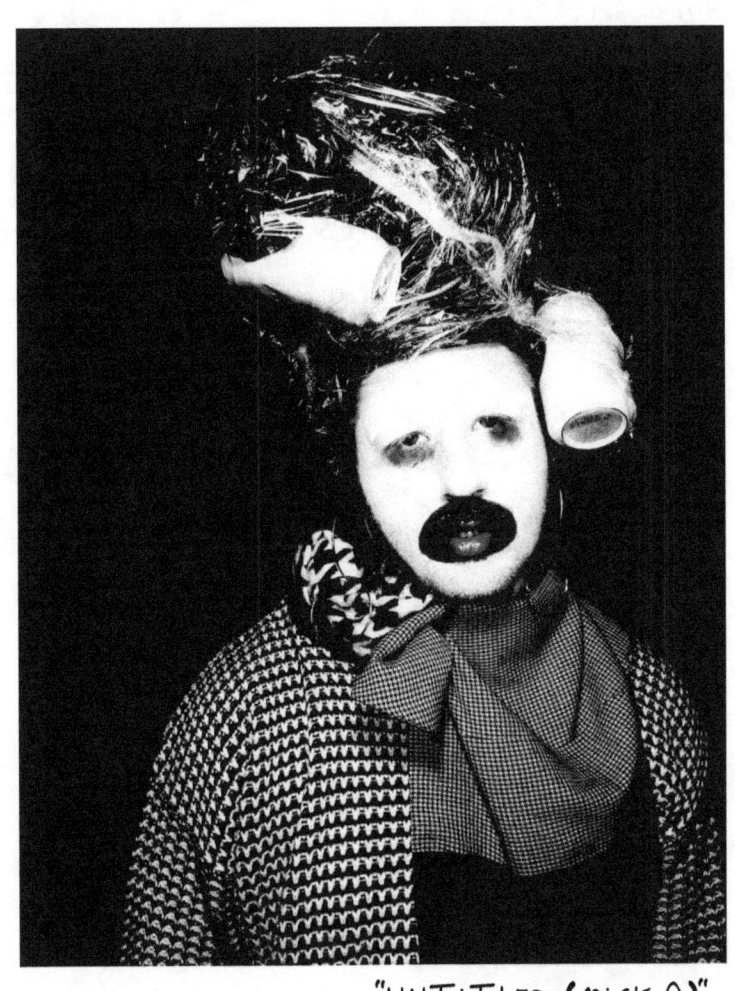
"UNTITLED (MICK Q)"
JULY 24 2017

JULY 22 2017
12:13 AM

i SMELL THE YELLOW.
HE CHANGES INTEGRITY
AGING BADLY
FEELING WORSE
THE LINING IS SLOWLY ERODING
AND i SEE THE YEARS OF YOUR FACE

RUNNING ALL THE REDS RUTHLESS, REELING
BLURRING BLOODY BULLETS DOWN MY CHEEKS

i LEFT MY CHOKER IN HIS BASEMENT
i LOST MY VIRGINITY IN HIS BEDROOM

HE'S NOT A POET HE'S A FRAUD
YET i'M FALLING IN LOVE WITH THE MOTION SICKNESS
AND YOU'VE GIVEN ME DISEASE

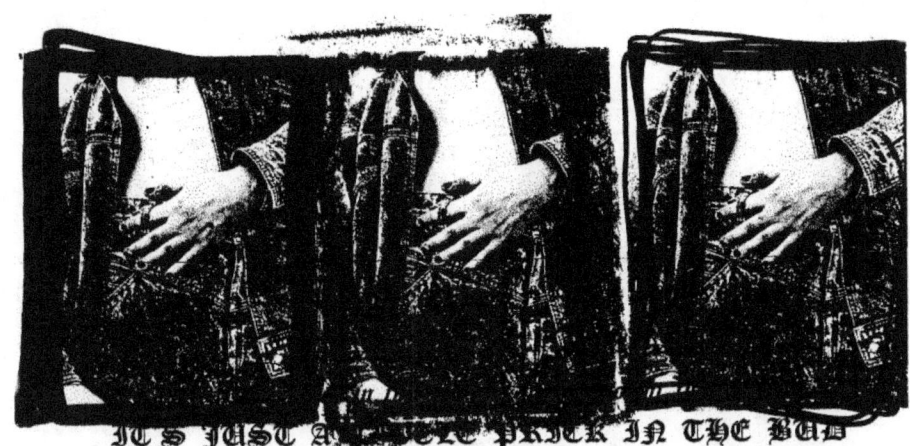

"NIGHTMARE IN ELSMERE"
JANUARY 25 2018

JULY 26 2017
7:55 AM

THEY SHOW ME THE SWANS AND THE SHRUBS
    AND THEIR HAIRY TORSO
AND ACQUAINT ME WITH THEIR POINTED LIPS

i SPEND THE NIGHT AND STAY AWAKE TO THE LOW
    WHIR OF THE AIR CONDITIONING UNIT AND THE
    SOFT HUM OF ALT ROCK
THINKING ABOUT EVERY PAIR OF LIPS THAT HAVE MET
    MINE

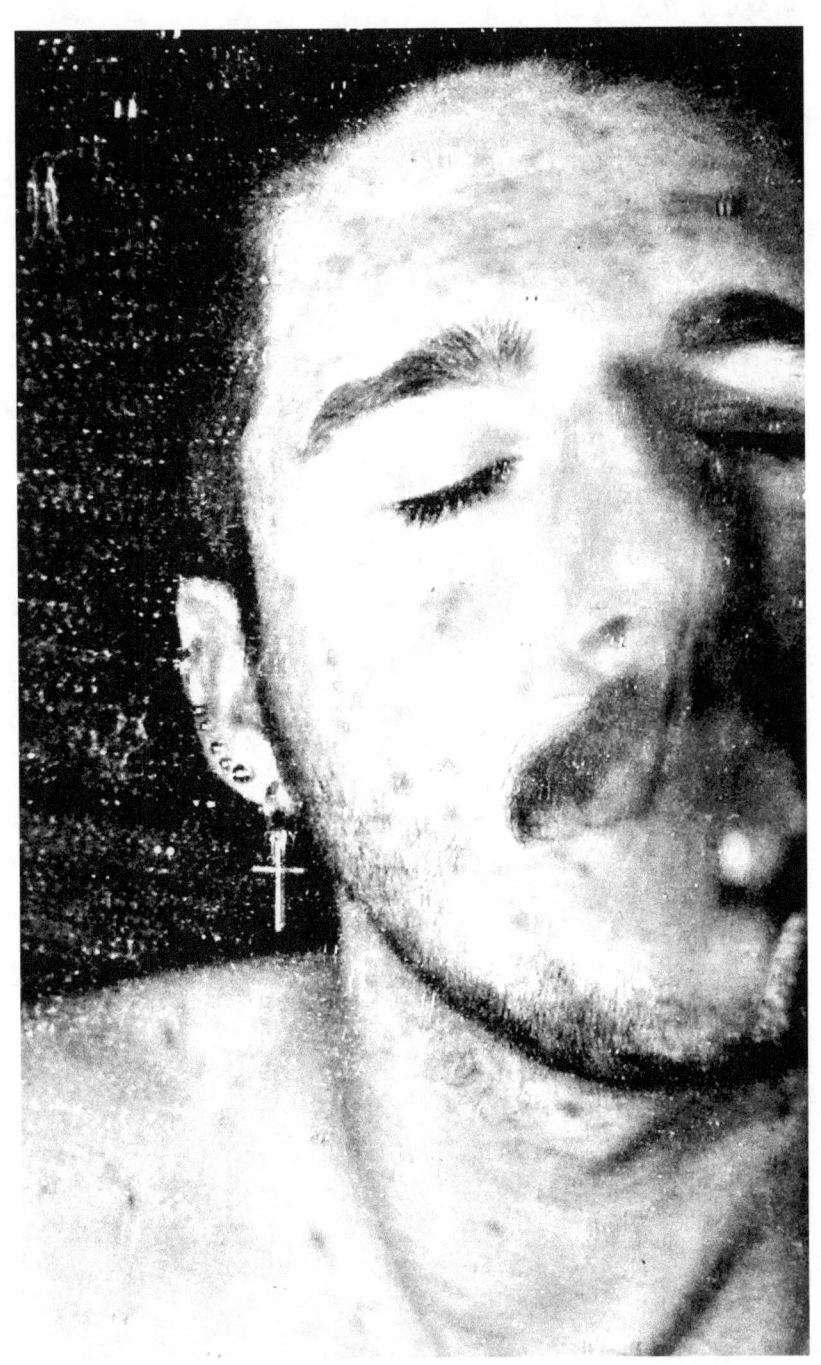

"i SPEND THE NiGHT iN THE ARBORETUM WiTH YOU" JULY 25 2017

JULY 28 2017
2:14 PM

PAPER CUPS PURPOSELY NONCHALANT IN NATURE
YET YOUR HANDS WRING MY THROAT LIKE A THIEF OF
    VISIONS
ROBBING ME OF MY YOUTH AND DIVIDING MY JOY
WARM SYRUP DOWN MY THIGHS UNWILLINGLY

I DIDN'T SEE YOU IN THE CITY
BUT YOU WERE DOWN THE STREET WITH ANOTHER

SHINING IS THE SUN IN THE CRYSTAL SHRINE
CONTRAST TO THE SMUG RIVERFRONT
I SCRATCH THE HICKEYS OFF MY NECK
AND CRY AT 3 AM IN ANOTHER'S BED
ESTRANGED FROM MYSELF UNDER YOUR OBLIVION

WHAT IS THE MEANING OF MY TEARS AND FEELS?
WHO IS AWARE OF THE DAMAGES CAUSED TO MY
    BURNING BODY?

SPARE ME THE STAINS
THE VERBALIZED AUTONOMY
REPETITIOUS BENDING
NOW THE GRAVITY STOMPS ON MY HEAD
LIKE THE WORLD COLLAPSED IN ON ME
AND IT DID AND YOU WATCHED AND PLEASURED
    YOURSELF
SPLATTERING THE WHITE LOVE STAIN

JULY 31 2017
1:08 PM

BLOOD STAINS ON BED SHEETS
LIPS NUMB FROM THE BITES

THIS BED A SWEATY SWIMMING POOL
HIS BODY DRENCHED IN DEEP

WE'RE BREEDING IN BETWEEN THE LINES AGAIN
AND IT'S ONLY PLEASURE IF WE BOTH FEEL IT

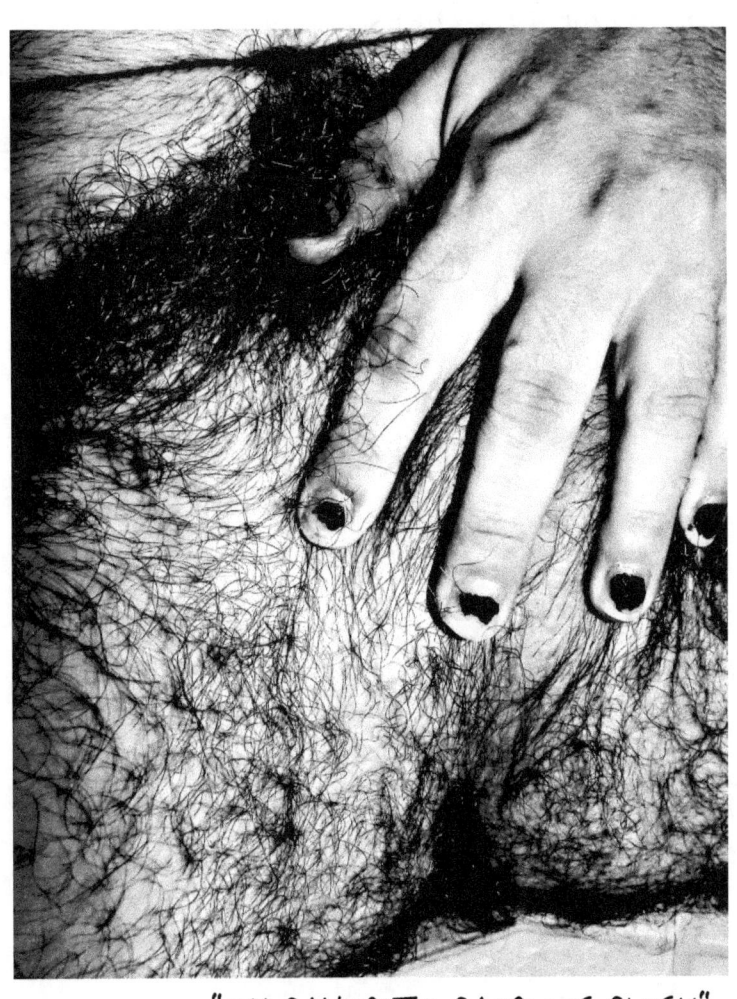

"MY FAVORITE FABRIC IS FLESH"
AUGUST 30 2017

AUGUST 1 2017
5:29 PM

A FALSE BEACON
YOU HAVE MORE THAN YOU NEED
SO I RECOIL THE CORDS
REINTRODUCE THE BLOODSHED
LET THE CORPSES DANCE

I PIERCE MY TONGUE DOWN ITS CENTER WITH HIS FORK
UNCONSCIOUS AND YOU'RE ANIMAL INTIMATE
THE SLURS ARE DROOLING AND THE SUICIDE IS
      TEMPTING

... GINA DIED IN 1990
AND I WILL DIE IN VAIN

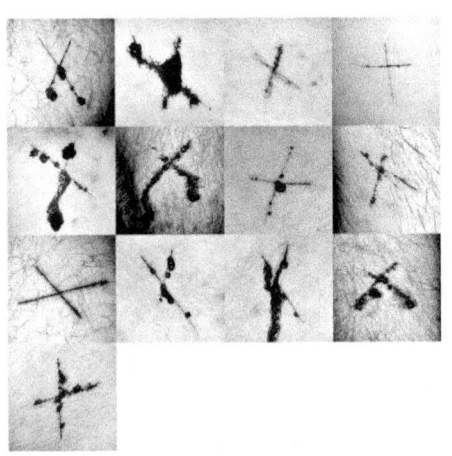 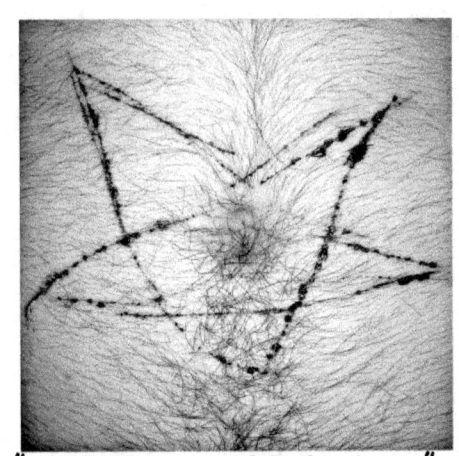

"UNTITLED PERFORMANCE"
JULY 28 - AUGUST 5 2017

AUGUST 11 2017
10:57 PM

i FEEL THE ROSE THORNS iN MY POCKETS AND
    SMELL THE LiQUOR ON YOUR BREATH
i WANT YOU AGAiN

i WANT TO TASTE THE SALiVA DRiPPiNG DOWN YOUR
    BEARDED CHiN AS YOU CLiMAX
SiT ON YOUR THiGHS HALF AWAKE HALF ORGASMED
FiLL YOU WiTH MY KiSSES AND TRACE EVERY GROOVE OF
    YOUR RiBS
BE THE ONLY ONE YOU LiVE iNSiDE
SMELL THE RUBBER BURNiNG AFTER WE FUCK

i FEEL THE VODKA iN MY EARS

AUGUST 15 2017
5:36 PM

i KiSS YOUR RiBS AND YOU FLiNCH
RETREAT FROM MY GENUiNE AFFECTiON
A FAR CRY FROM THE OLD PASSiON WE SHARED
NOW YOU WON'T EXCHANGE A GLANCE

MUSCLE HYSTERiA
WiTH THE HEART CHORDS FiERY
i WAS THE CORPSE YOU COULDN'T CARRY

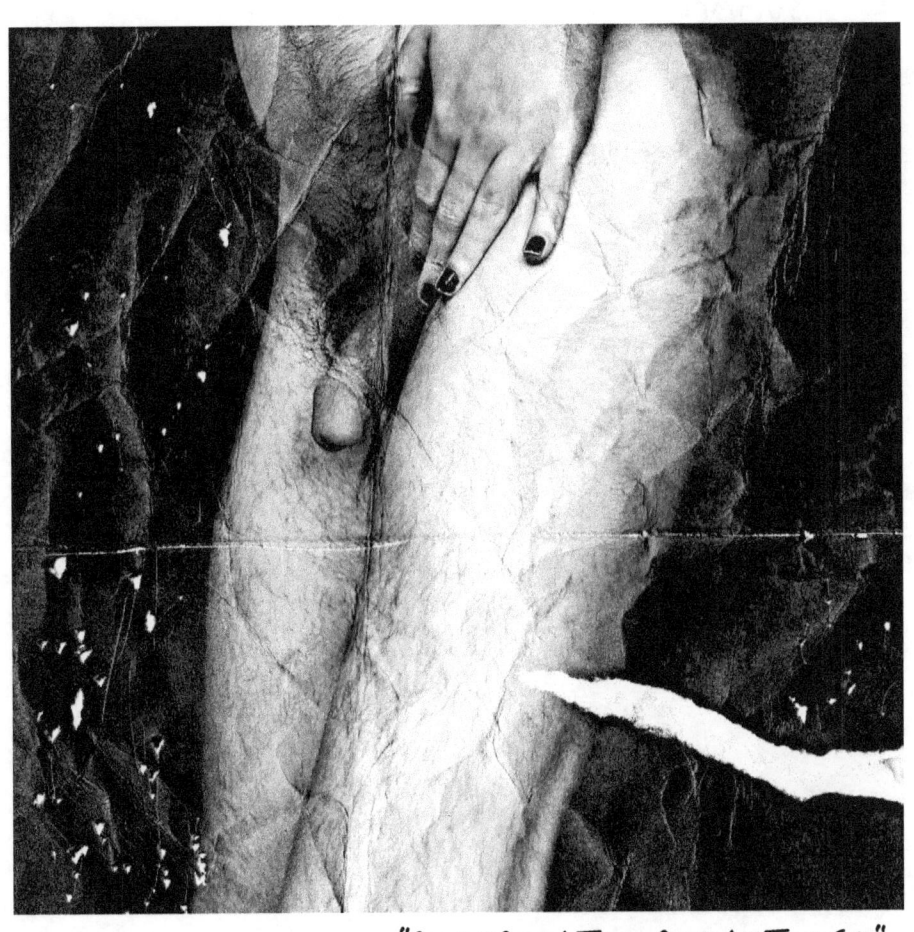

"RECIPROCATED ROMANTICISM"
DECEMBER 27 2017

AUGUST 27 2017
1:51 PM

PERMANENTLY FURROWED BROW WITH THE FURIED
    FORESKIN TO MATCH
OUR BODIES OVERLAPPING IN THE SAME NEW YORK CITY
    SUMMER
WITHOUT AIR CONDITIONING
WITHOUT WORDS
WITHOUT A NODE OF A NERVE
WE SANK INTO YOUR SHEETS AND STAYED CLOSE
UNTIL WE DRIFTED FAR

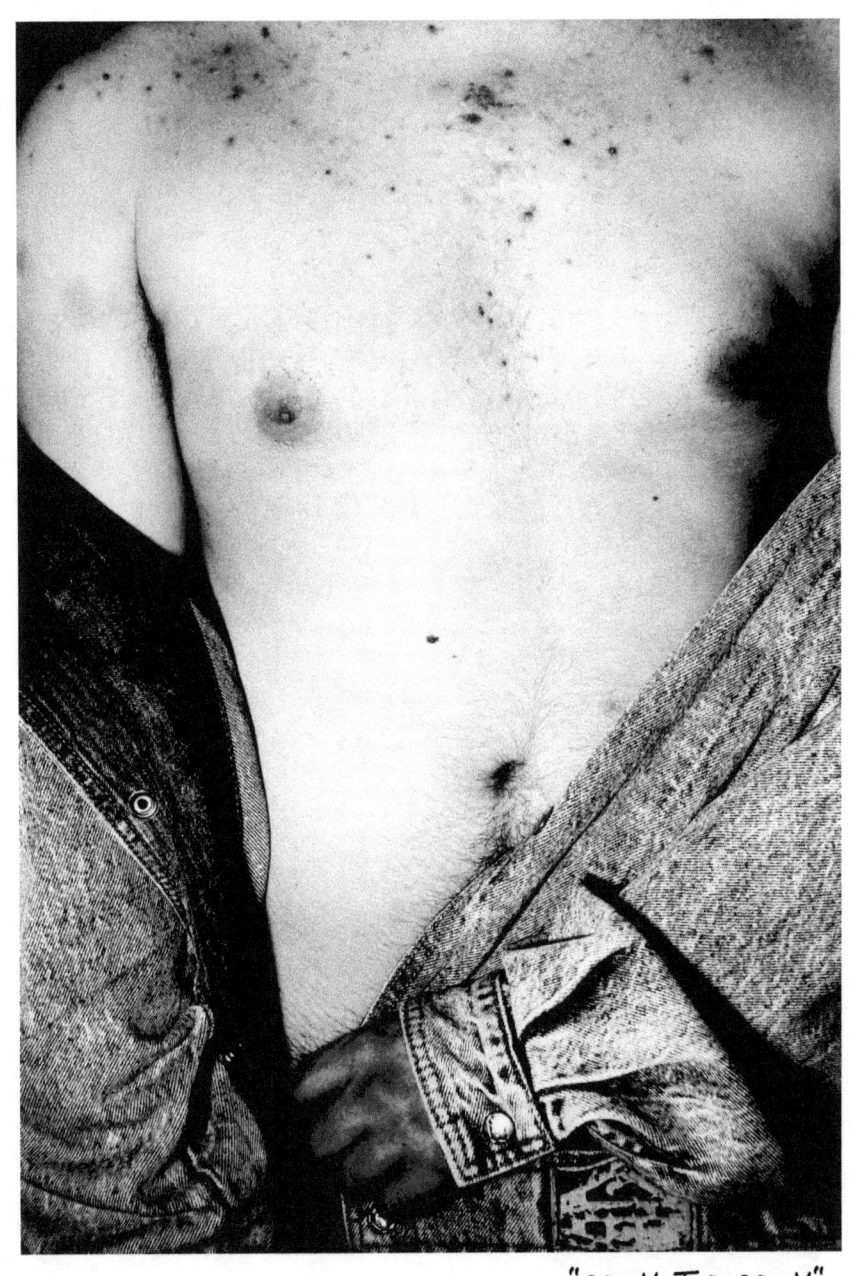

"BODY TO BODY"
FEBRUARY 22 2017

AUGUST 31 2017
8:32 PM

WAS HER FIRST LOVE HER LAST?
SHE'S STANDING ON THE SHOULDER OF SELF
    DESTRUCTION
WITH VEINS BURSTING FROM THEIR CORRESPONDING EYE
    SOCKETS

AND ALL THE BOYS SHE'S EVER KISSED TOOK PIECES OF
    HER WITH THEM WHEN THEY LEFT
AND HER PALMS ARE SWEATY AND HER GAZE IS HEAVY
    AND HER ECHOES HIT THE SHALLOW WALLS
THE STOLEN MOMENTS AND CRIMES MAKE HER MELT
    AWAY IN MISERY OF YESTERDAY

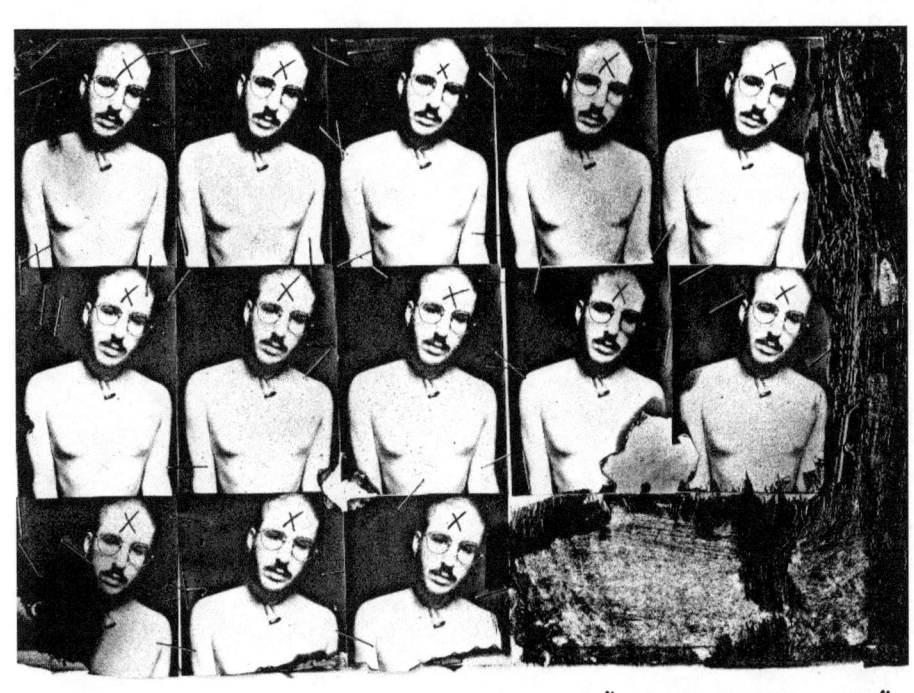

SEPTEMBER 5 2017
12:23 AM

YOU'RE IN EVERY ROOM I ENTER
A MILKY GHOST
CHASING MY GAZE
BLANKETING ME IN REGRET

GLASS IN THE GUMS
OF A TIGER
LOOKING TO FEED

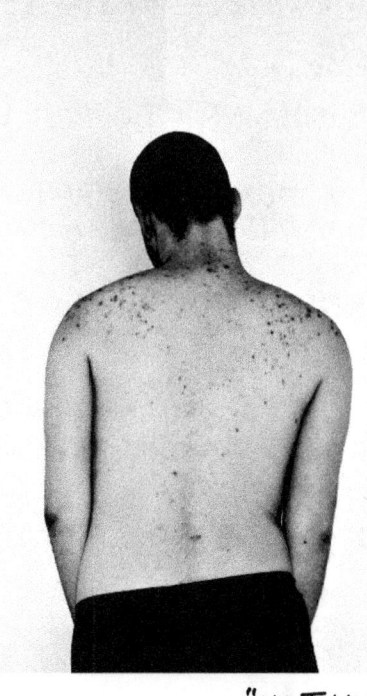

"NOTHING SUBTLE"
JULY 27 2017

SEPTEMBER 14 2017
2:21 PM

LICK THE SWEAT FROM HIS BROW AND RECITE THE
    RHYTHM
DUMB WITH SOURBONE DRUNKNESS WILTING AT THE
    SIGHT
WRITHING ON LIMESTONE ALTARS
FEELING YOUR CHAINSAW COMMOTION
BETWEEN MY LEGS

SALTY SKY TANGIBLE IN MY BLIND EYE BREATHING
    CYCLE
FOGGING THE FRAMES
MELTING AND MOLDING INTO YOUR USELESS EMBRACE I'M
    YOURS
ONLY IN THE MOMENT YOU WANT ME
ONLY THE MOMENT YOU CALL MY NAME

TOWERING OVER MY LIMP BODY WITH A CROOKED TABLE
    GRIN
INTO THE SOFT DRINK SUNSET
DULLNESS IN THE COCKROACH HEAVEN
COLLECTING KISSES RUNNING BACKWARDS ON EMPTY
    CARELESS CONTACT
FOR MY CONTEMPORARY APPETITES

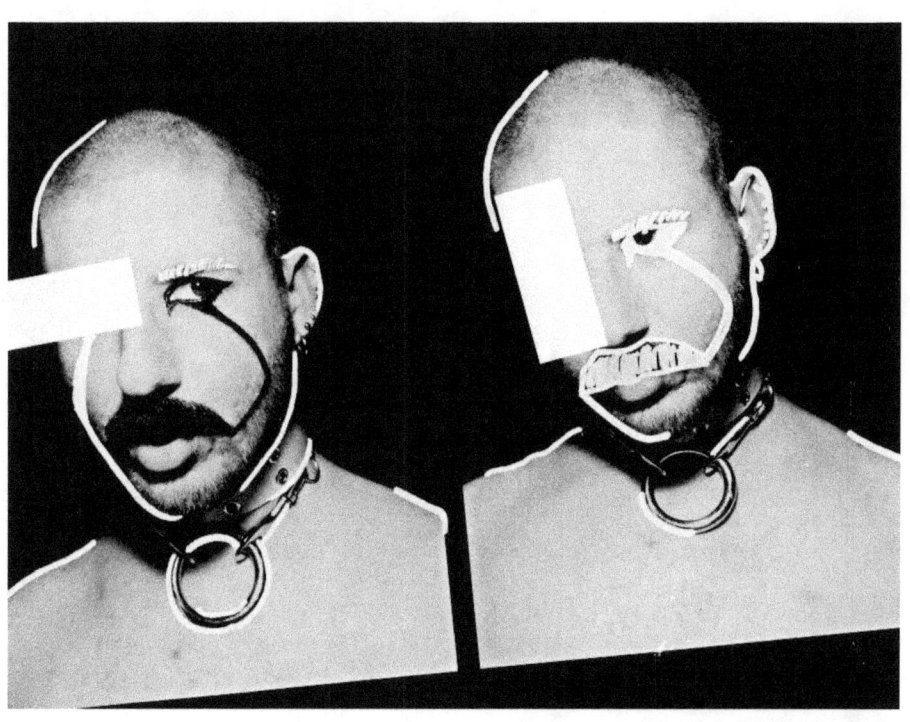

"WE COULD BE FUCKING"
AUGUST 29 2017

SEPTEMBER 19 2017
11:59 AM

i LAY CATATONIC LiKE A CORPSE ON YOUR COUCH iN THE
    BASEMENT
PALE FLESHED AND FLUSHED CHEEKS
LiFELESS LiKE YOU LiKE ME TO BE
OH THE DiRTY GUMMED, NiCOTiNE TASTED HOT AiR

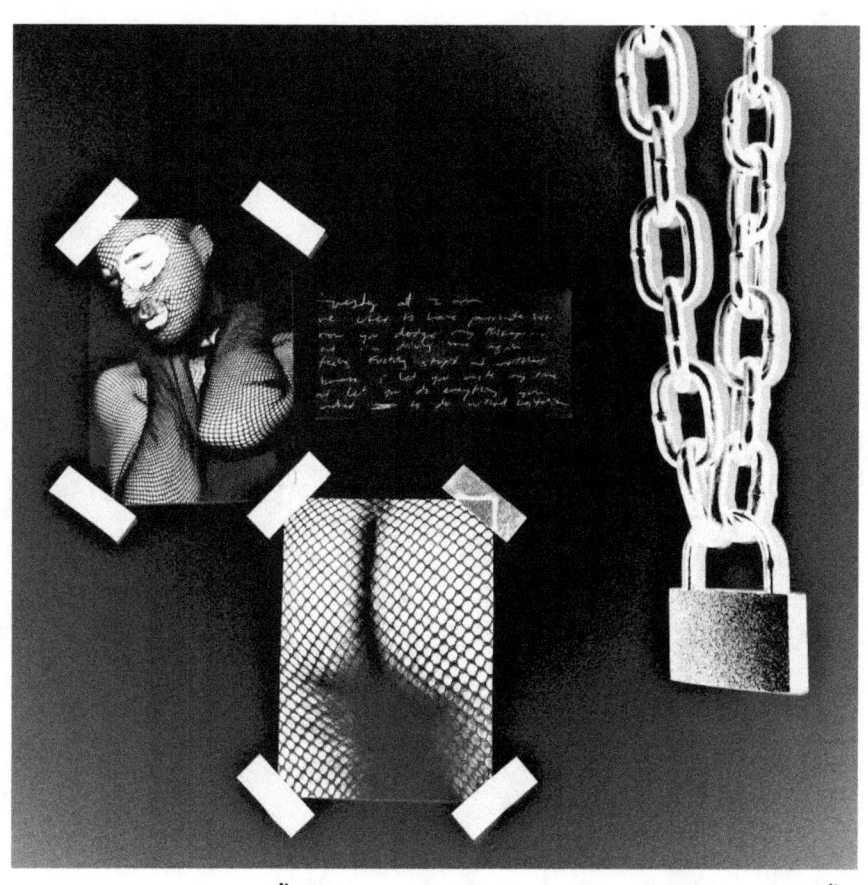

"THE CORPSE YOU COULDN'T CARRY"
AUGUST 19 2017

OCTOBER 4 2017
12:00 AM

HE PIERCED HIS EAR IN SAINT MARK'S PLACE TO MATCH
    MINE
BLED FOR AN HOUR BUT WOULDN'T LET ME LICK THE
    BLOOD
ARGUED IN BROOKLYN STREETS ON A RAINY DAY
SAT IN SILENCE IN OUR FAVORITE THRIFT STORE
    DOWNTOWN
ATE A PLATE OF LO MEIN IN MANHATTAN
    AND MY ASS IN HIS DORM ROOM UNDER THE
    COVERS.
BOUGHT ME TSHIRTS AND STOOD CROSS ARMED IN
    ART MUSEUMS
LET HIS TEETH TASTE MY NECK IN LONG ISLAND ON
    HIS PULL OUT BED
WATCHED ME CRY FOR AN HOUR AND WALKED WITH ME
    FORTY BLOCKS TO THE BUS RIDE HOME
SHOWERED WITH EMPTY SHAMPOO BOTTLES AT OUR
    FEET
TRIED TO PUT CONDOMS ON OUR FLACCID COCKS ON
    THE BATHROOM FLOOR
TOUCHED TONGUES OUTSIDE THE TACO BELL ON 97TH
    STREET
THEN YOU TOLD ME THAT YOU LOVED ME

10:01 PM

HE WORE MY PUBIC HAIR ON HIS FACE
USED HIS TONGUE AS A SPOON
TO EAT THE FLESHY CUNT
NECK WET FROM THE TEARS
SABOTAGED LOVELESS EYES
DRIED BLOOD TURNS BROWN
AND YOU LET IT COME TO THIS

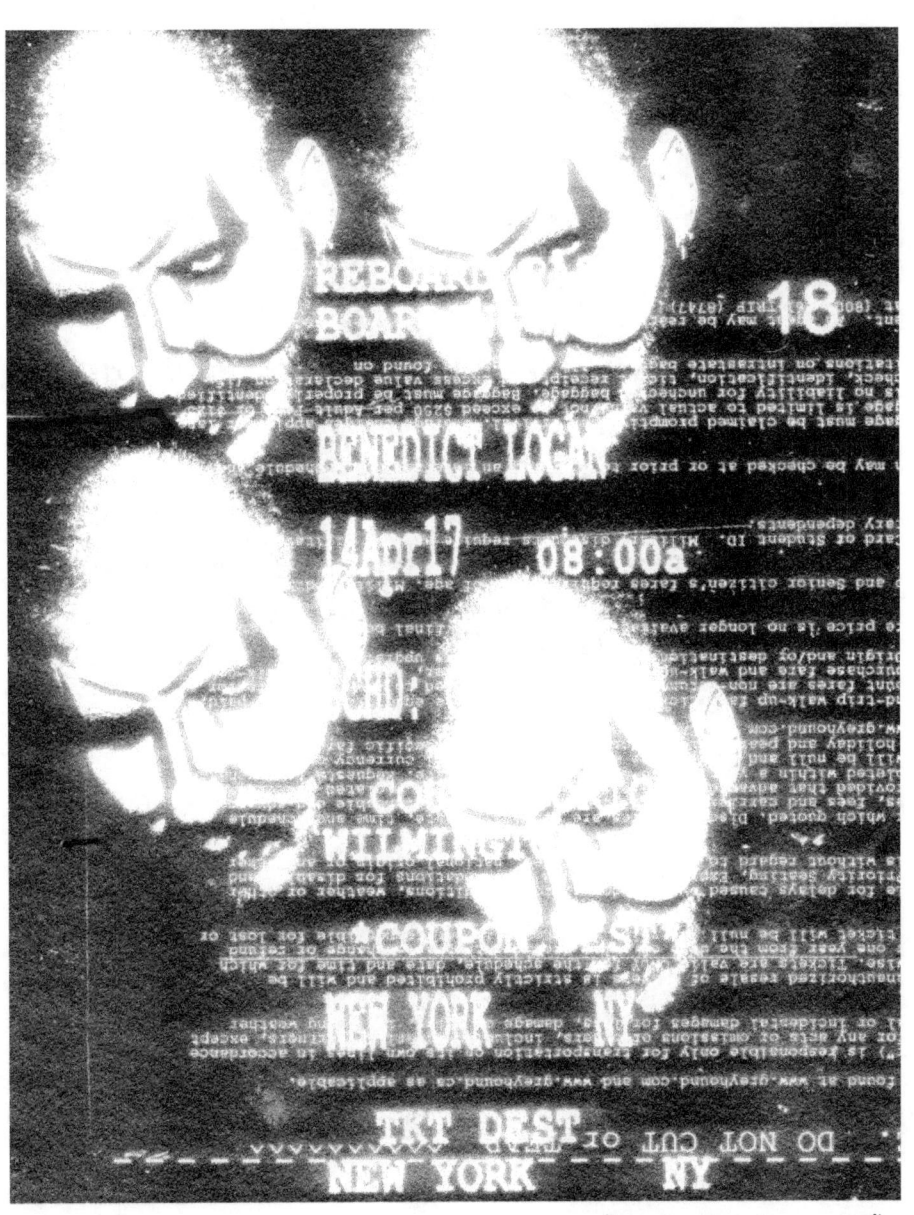

"CARPETFUCKING"
JUNE 2 2017

OCTOBER 29 2017
7:40 PM

AND THE WORLD TURNS TO A WET MOSAIC
AND MY VISION IS SKEWED DRENCHED
AND I'M DRIVING HOME BLIND

WE STARED DEEPLY INTO EACH OTHER'S EYES
    AND HIS IGNITED IN FAST PROGRESSION
I FELT HIS WEIGHT LOWER ON ME AND REMEMBERED I
    WAS NOT HIS OWN
I AM NOT HIS OWN LOVER BUT ANOTHER TOUCH HE
    DEMANDS TO FEEL

HE'S VANISHED INTO THE BACK OF MY MIND
GONE LIKE THE BLOOD BEHIND MY EARS
AND HE'S HAPPIER WITHOUT ME, WITH HIMSELF AND
    HIS POSSESSIONS IN HIS APARTMENT IN HIS CITY
    WITH HIS HUSBAND

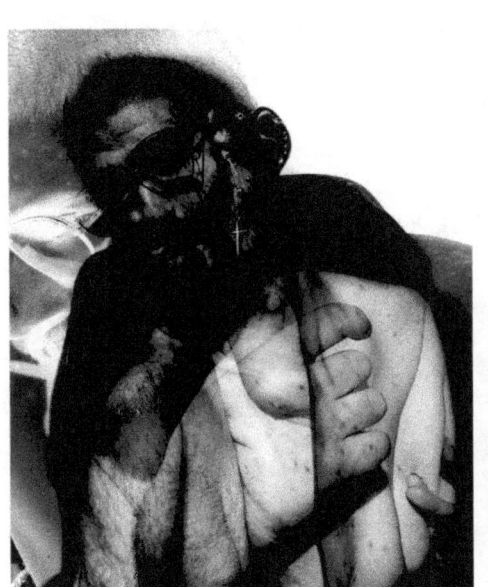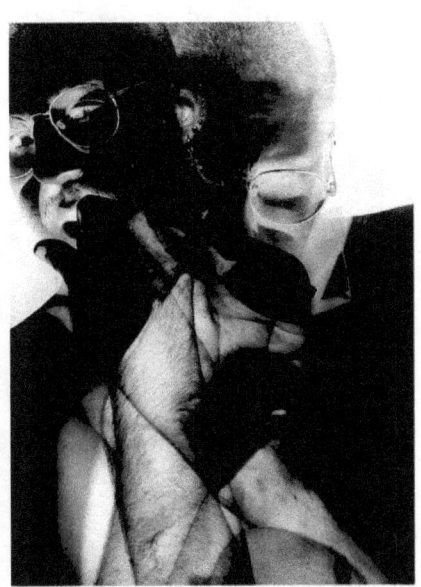

"WHY DID YOU TURN THE LIGHTS OFF AS I WAS UNDRESSING?" JULY 31 2017

NOVEMBER 1 2017
9:28 PM

AS THE ROCKS GROW HEAVIER IN MY WET POCKETS I
    DIP MY HANDS INTO THE SANDS TO SIFT FOR
    THE TREASURES
IT SEEMS THAT BLACK COFFEE DOESN'T TASTE THE
    SAME
AND THE DAYS PASS WITHOUT MY SAY
AND THE ATTIC IS HOTTER THAN EVER
AND WHO WILL POLISH THESE STONES IF I DON'T?

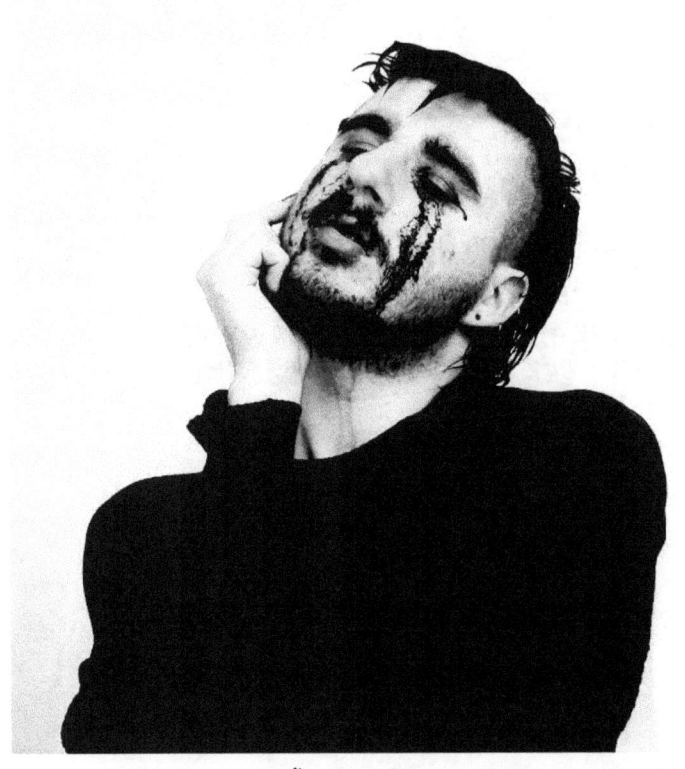
"UNTITLED (BLACK TEARS)"
MARCH 1 2017

NOVEMBER 2 2017
2:44 PM

DRUNK ON THE RED IRON
HE'S MY LUCRATIVE LOVER AND I'M HIS WHORE
HIS SHADOW OF RELEASE
HIS WOLF SUPPER

I'M RIDING HIS COCK UNTIL I BLEED AGAIN IN DEEP
    REGRET

NOVEMBER 3 2017
9:56 PM

I MISS THE WAY YOUR HANDS MET MY THIGHS WITH
    SUCH COOL ABANDON
AND YOUR DRUNK TONGUE SAW MY FEET
THE HUNGER YOU POSSESSED WHEN YOU SAW A MEAL
    TO EAT

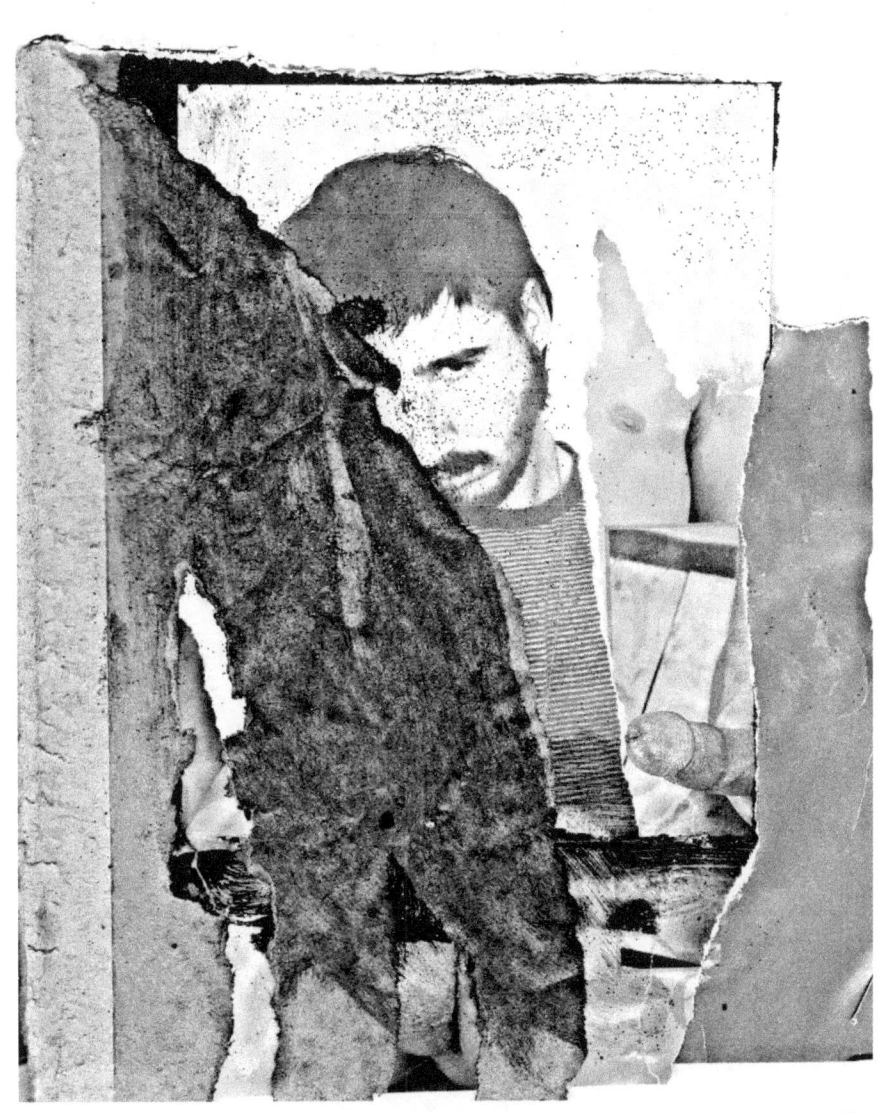

"UNTITLED (WHAT WOULD AN ANGEL SAY?)"
FEBRUARY 12 2017

NOVEMBER 16 2017
2:16 PM

RESTING ON YOUR SHOULDER BLADE
I'M MORE THAN A BODY COLLIDED
IN YOUR LUNGS COMES THE BREATH OF AN ANGELIC
    ENTITY
WET WITH EXCITEMENT, GRAZING EYES LONGING FOR A
    LONGER STAY
THE SILKY CHANTEUSE USING HER CHORDS TO REVIVE

SO THE RAPTURE SEEMS UNDESTINED
AND YOU SEEM LIKE YOU'RE MINE

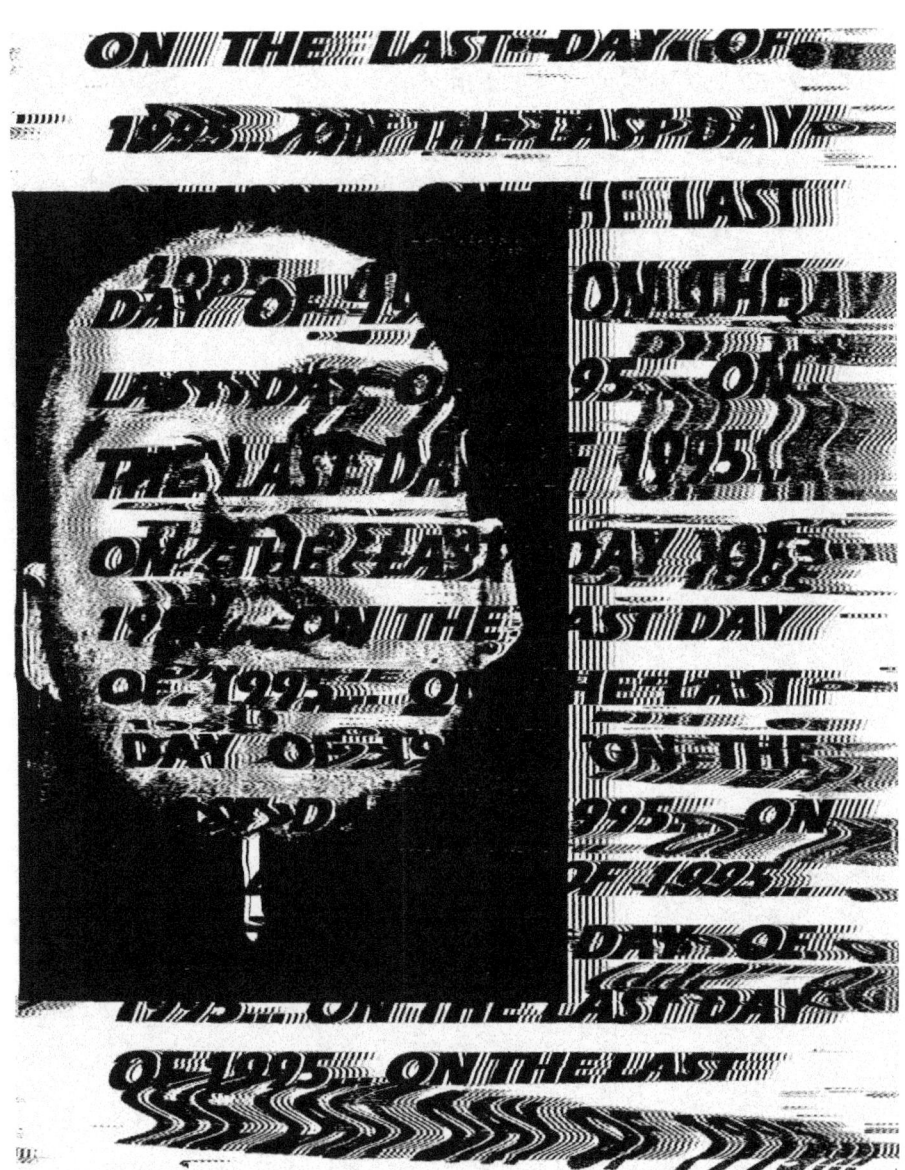

"NAKED LIKE MY ALIBI (ON THE LAST DAY OF 1995)" DECEMBER 30 2017

NOVEMBER 17 2017
4:24 PM

HE BLOODIED UP MY KNEES
AND LOCKED ME TO THE AIR MATTRESS TO DO AS HE
    DESIRED
i CRY iN CLOSE PROXIMITY, NAUSEOUS
HELLISH BOY i CAN FEEL HIS HORNS FINGERING MY BLOODY
    GASHES WITH HIS LONG INFECTED SILVER ROD
i'M VOMITING IN HIS BEDROOM NAKED ON MY HANDS AND
    KNEES PULSING BEGGING PLEADING
BUT THAT DIDN'T STOP HIM

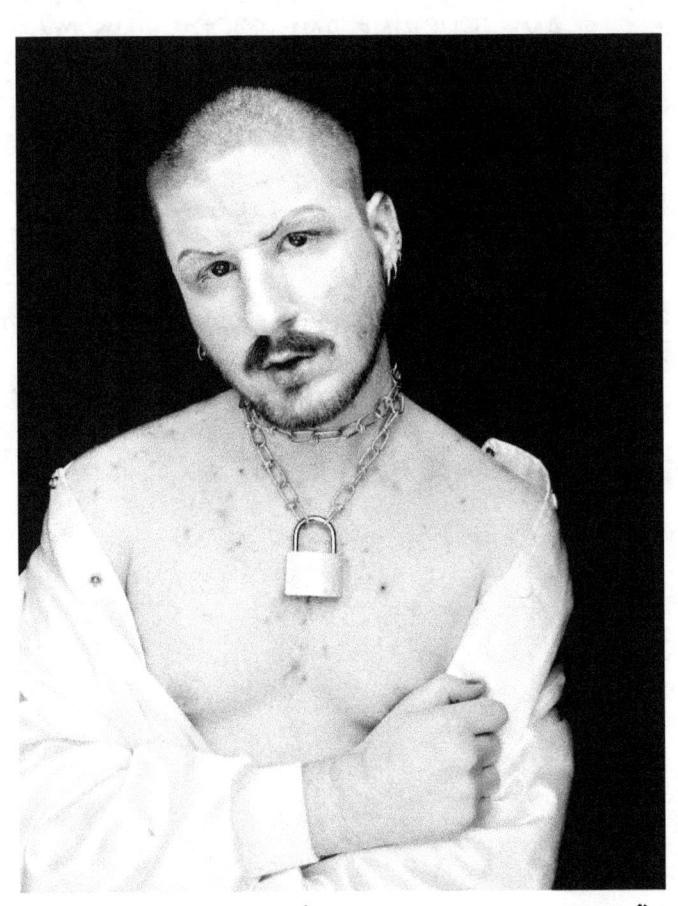

"FREEDOM IS ELASTIC"
JUNE 3 2017

NOVEMBER 22 2017
12:45 AM

MY TIRES KISS THE HIGHWAY SO EASY, SO SMOOTH
I DRIVE ALONE ON THESE DESERTED ROADWAYS BUT
    THEY'RE POLLUTED BY ISOLATED VOCALS OF WIND
      AND TURBINE AND STEEL AND MECHANICAL LUST
AND THEY SCREAM SO LOUD

DECEMBER 16 2017
12:23 AM.

NOSEDIVING INTO A KISS ON YOUR REAR VIEW
SWEATY METAL ALLOY STENCH
KEEPING THE KNOTS STRAIGHT AND THE JOYED
    TEARS WET
EASILY GOING 85 ON 80 EAST

HOT COFFEE COLD FISH
HE WEARS YOUR AFTERSHAVE AND MY TRAITOR SMILE
HAZY LIKE A BLACK SUMMER FIST

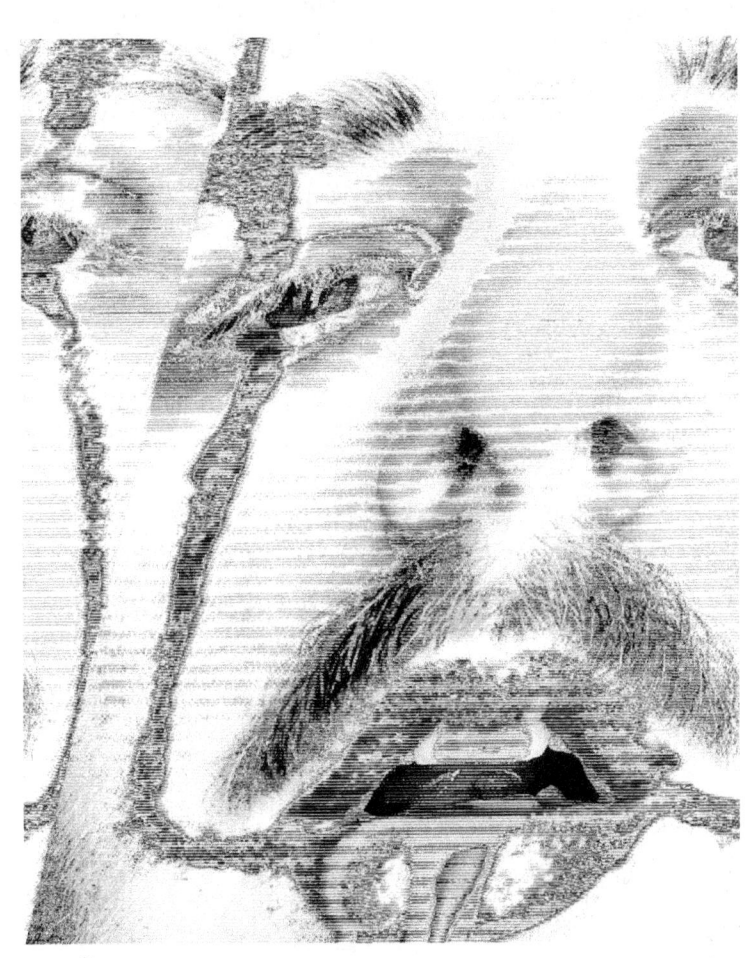

"EVEN ON THE LONGEST DAY MY HUNGER FOR HIM IS INSATIABLE" DECEMBER 27 2017

JANUARY 16 2018
4:47 PM

INHALING THE INSIDES OF ME
ALL IS SILENT BESIDES HEAVY BREATHING
MUFFLED MOANS AND PAINED PANTS AND CRIES
ALL IS STICKY SEMEN GUTTER TEARS TRAUMA TRASH
    LEATHER
CARPETFUCKING ME LIKE THE BEAST WITHIN
YOUR MILK SPIKED AND SOILED DRIPPING DOWN MY CHIN
MY BLISTERED BRUISED PEACH SCREAMING AND OOZING
    HIS JUICE

JANUARY 17 2018
10:29 AM

LIKE A CHOKEHOLD
LEFT BUT IT WILL LINGER LOUDER
LOST BUT STRANGER THAN STRONG
BECAUSE EVERY FETISH IS A FALLACY

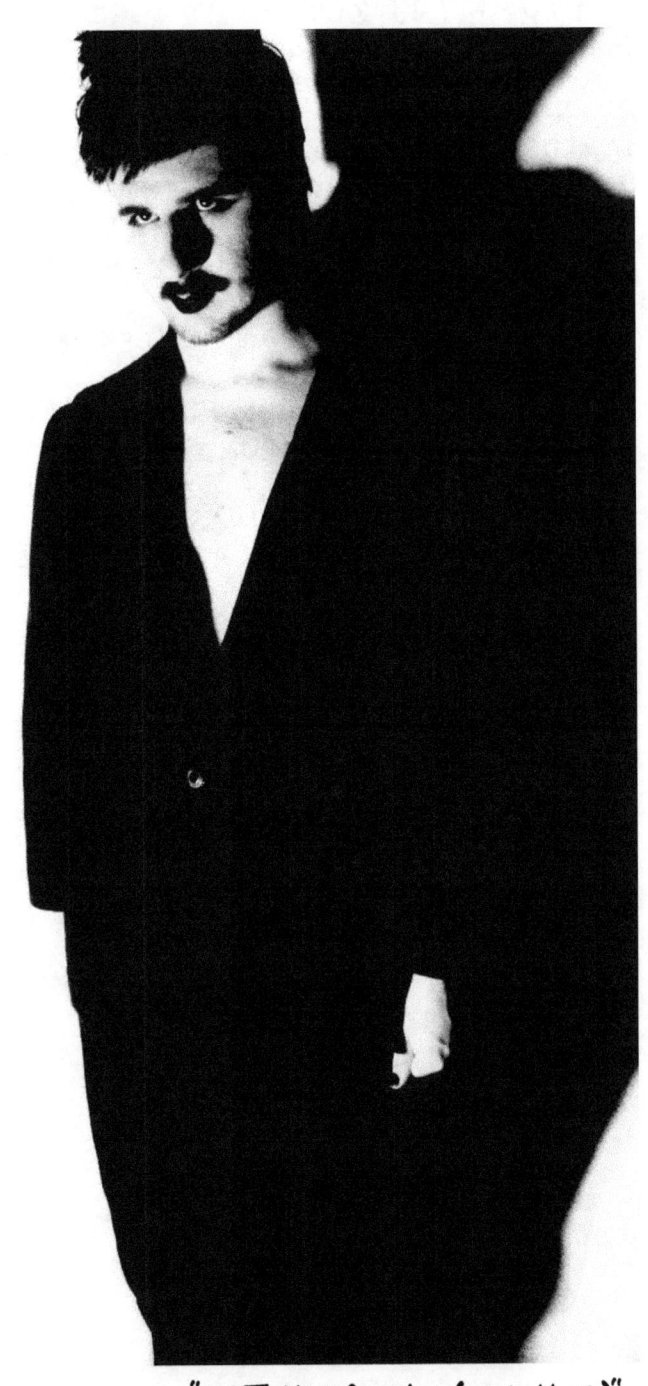

"NOT YOUR MAN (CINDY 112)"
FEBRUARY 1 2017

JANUARY 18 2018
11:30 AM

I'M JUST THE BODY YOU INHABITED FOR SIX MONTHS
THE HOME YOU ROBBED EMPTY
THE CUNT YOU BRED BLOODY BATTERED
THE BOVINE BREAKFAST YOU CONSUMED

AND THERE IS BLOOD IN MY UNDERWEAR
AND YOU PUT IT THERE
AND WE WERE STRANGERS FUCKING RAW
AND YOU KNEW THE WOUND WAS FRESH YET STILL
    INFLICTED THE TRAUMA
AND YOU KNEW THE SOUNDS WERE PAIN RIDDEN YET
    STILL YOU GRINDED ATOP MY AGONIZED MARBLE
    CAST OF A BODY

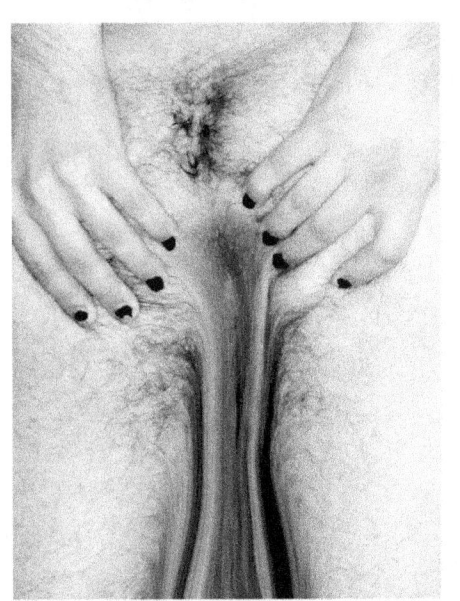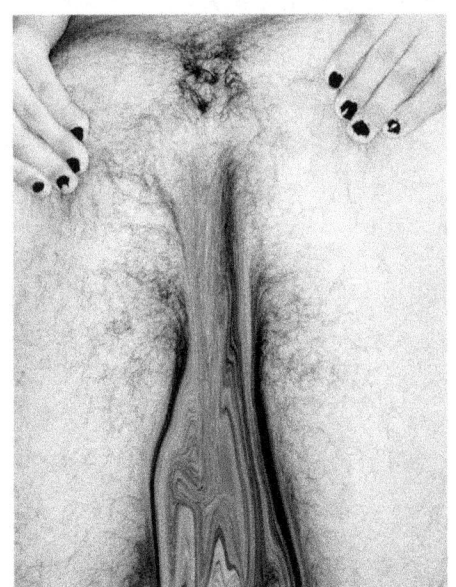

"RED ATLAS"
AUGUST 26 2017

JANUARY 23 2018
12:46 PM

NIGHTMARE IN ELSMERE
EDGING ON ELSEWHERE
FORCEFULLY STRIPPED NAKED FOR YOUR URGES AND
    VIOLENT PLEASURES
AND I NEVER SAID YES

BLESSED ARE THOSE WHO EAT NOTHING BUT DIRT
WHOSE FACES ARE MASHED WITH FISTS AND CONCRETE
LEGS SLICED AND CUT FROM BARBED WIRE WALKING
WHOSE HEARTS ARE FULL OF ICE BUT BODIES BATTERED
    WITH BRUISES
THE ABUSED AND THE ANGELS ARE ONE OF THE SAME
I AM SO SORRY

JANUARY 24 2018
3:48 PM

WE WERE BORN STILL
WITH WATER IN OUR ENGINES
AND TREPIDATION COATING OUR LUNGS IN ASH
CRASSNESS ERRATIC
WITH ROACHES CRAWLING AROUND OUR HEAD SPACES
VERBAL IRONY UNPRONOUNCED
NEGATIVE IMBALANCE JUST TO SATISFY

BLEEDING THROUGH OUR SKIRTS ONTO STRANGER'S LAPS
THROWING OUR BODIES TO THE WOLVES WHO WANTED
    NOTHING BUT FLESH TO CHEW
CARELESS CONTACT AND LAZIER LUST GLOSSY AND
    STICKY
STRUNG OUT ON STRIFE AND DRY RYE
DRINKING NOTHING BUT TRAUMA TONICS AND
    ANTIDEPRESSANT SMOOTHIES
POOR FOR THE SALT OF THE EARTH'S STRUGGLES

...AND MY CORE WILL BLEED PINK LAVA FROM MY
    RECTUM UNTIL i COME TO PEACE WITH THE
    THINGS YOU'VE DONE TO ME WITHOUT
    PERMISSION

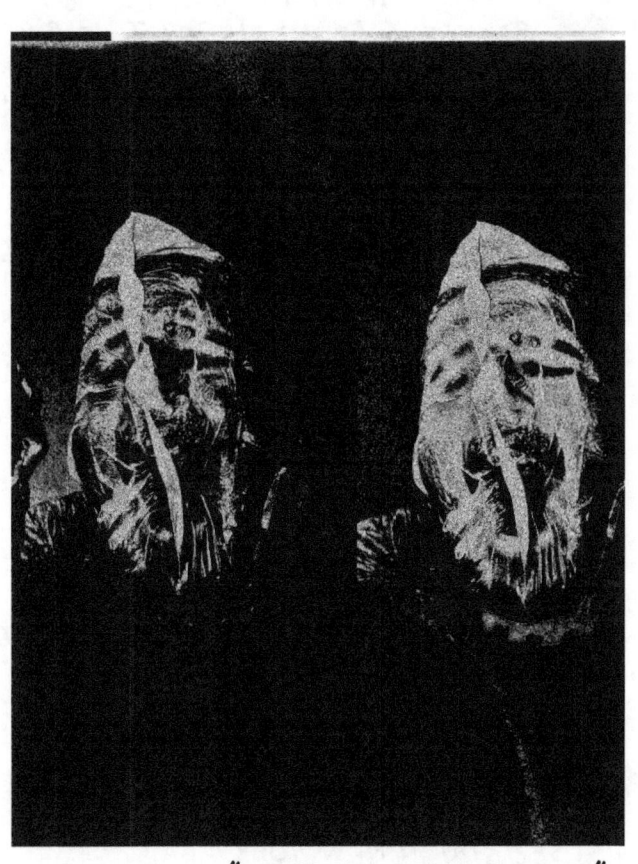

"WATER IN THE ENGINE"
JANUARY 30 2018

JANUARY 24 2018
4:47 PM

i still taste the one sided secret love affair
the stale air of subway fares and greyhound
    drives
i remember the way your lips met my flesh with
    reckless abandon for the first time
those molars pinching my ass cheeks
i had undying passion for my first love but he did
    not hold me tight enough
the bones cracked under the newer weight

i can forfeit the new york city nights
if only you'd quit the chase
the city is not ours any longer
the time we spend was sacred, true, but long
    gone now

JANUARY 28 2018
11:32 PM

i will sleep in a five foot crawlspace
live off hot coffee and cold fish
to open my eyes again
for a fighting chance
bash my skull with the bricks if need be
if failure falls
if i see you in new york again

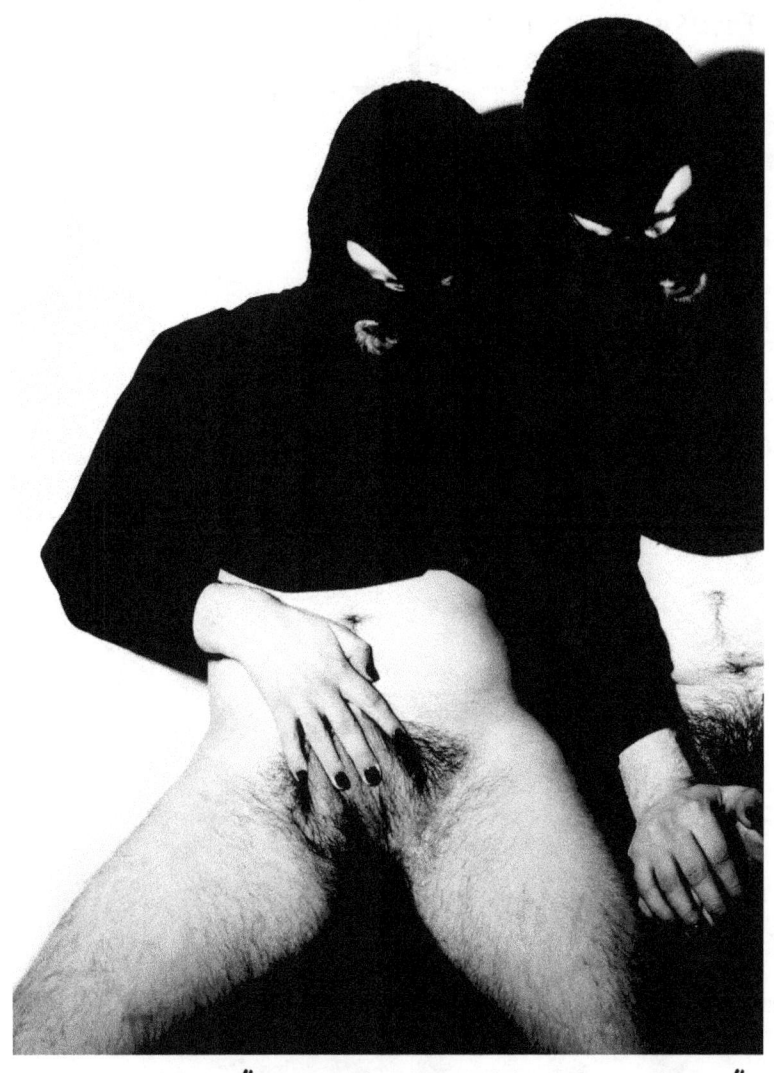

FEBRUARY 7 2018
8:17 PM

AND HE SEES VISIONS
BEYOND THE YELLOW INCISORS
THOSE LANKY LIMBS AND
GREASE FIRE FIXTURES
I HAVE ARRIVED TO TASTE YOUR YOLK FROM MY
    DREAMS
AND THE SKY IS AS ANTICIPATED

MY ROUGH THUMBS
MEET YOUR PINK LEAVES
AND WE FALL TOGETHER
INTO FEATHERS
AND I'M SMILING
FOR THE FIRST TIME
IN A LONG TIME

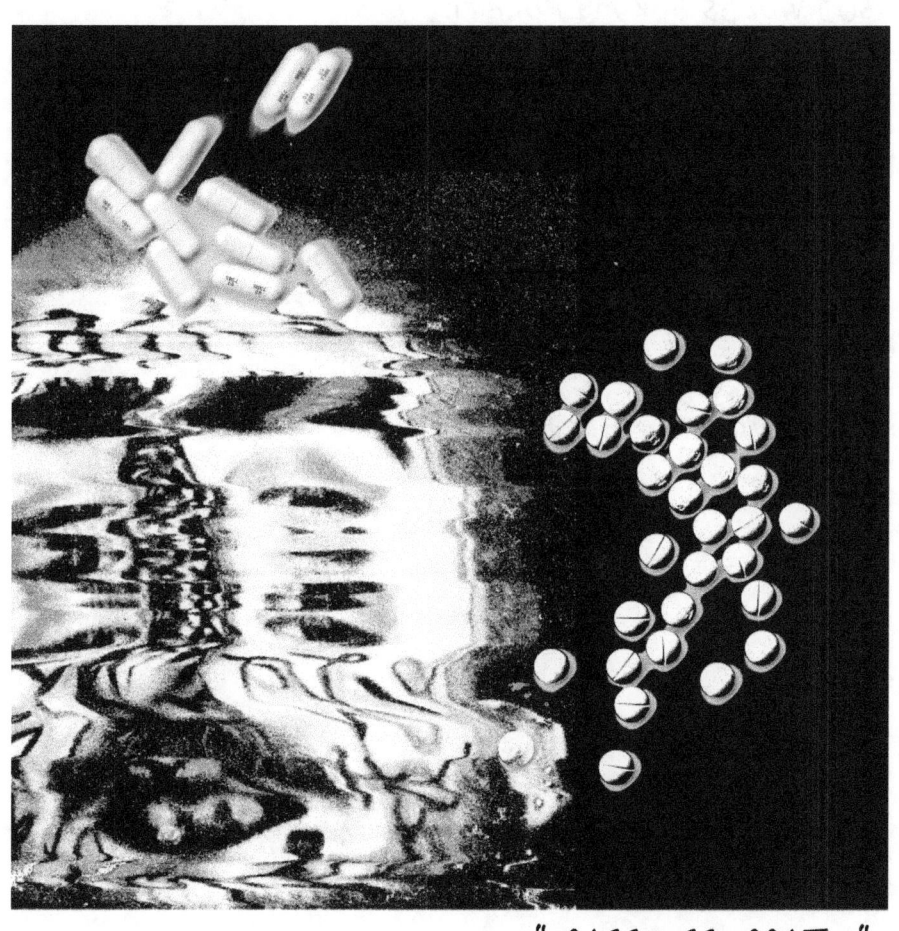

"CRASSNESS ERRATIC"
DECEMBER 29 2017

FEBRUARY 27 2018
12:29 AM

HOW ABOUT INTIMACY WITHOUT CONTROL?
3500 WORDS FOR MY FORMER
IN CEMENT INTO THE AFTERLIFE

I DON'T NEED HIS ARMS ON ME TO KNOW
HE'S THE ONLY ONE I CAN PEACEFULLY SLEEP BESIDE

WHEN ULTIMACY IS CAREFUL
HUNGER IS PRUDENT
COLOR ME CAREFUL NOWADAYS

FIVE HANDS ON THE ROSARY
WATCHING THE MARBLE FLOAT

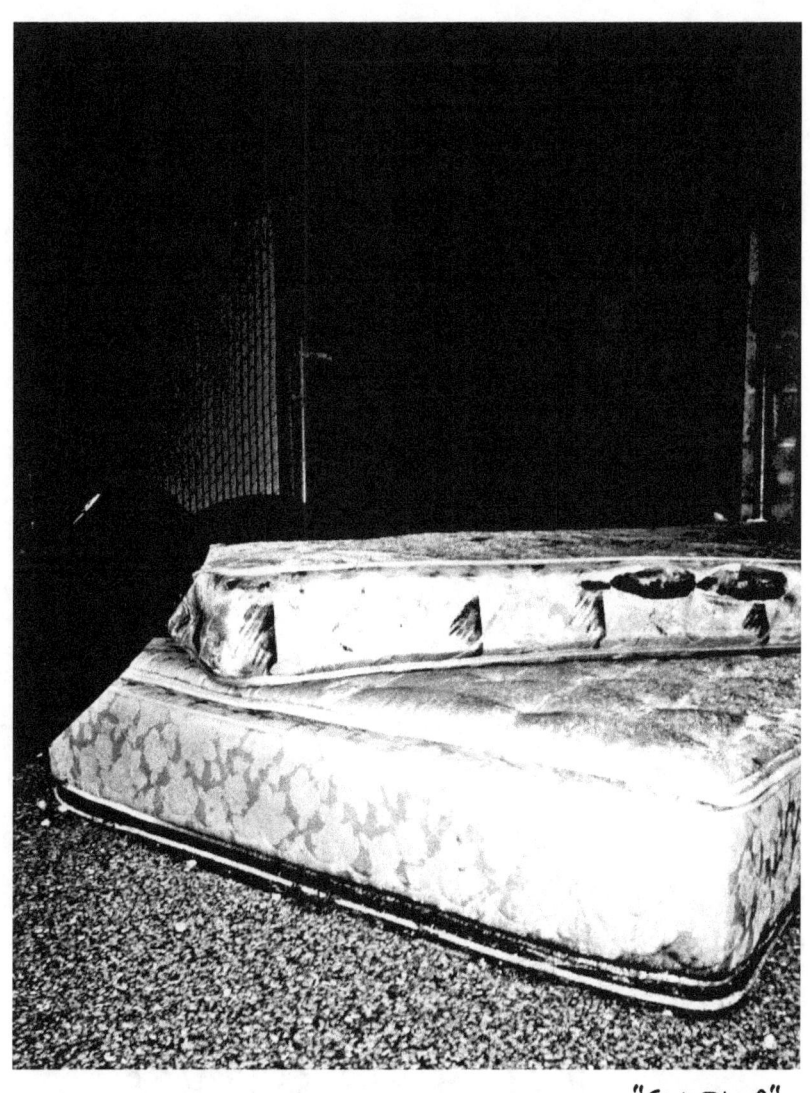

"SIMPLER"
MARCH 6 2017

pick your culture
LB 1997
artbyloganbenedict.com

www.ingramcontent.com/pod-product-compliance
Lightning Source LLC
Chambersburg PA
CBHW070204230526
45471CB00002B/808